HAPPY LIFE BLUES

A Memoir of Survival

Cecily Mattocks Marshall

Angus MacGregor Books, 75 Green Street, P.O. Box 968, Clinton MA 01510.

First Edition

Printed on Cougar Opaque acid free paper.

Library of Congress Control Number: **2007908173**

ISBN 13: 978-0-9790598-7-2
ISBN 10: 0-9790598-7-9

07 08 09 10   AMB/DCI   9 8 7 6 5 4 3 2 1

Cover design: Cynthia Hall Marshall

DEDICATED TO MY PARENTS
Whose legacy serves as inspiration for my family…
and the generations to follow.

People will not look forward to posterity
who never looked backward to their ancestors.
Reflections on the Revolution in France
Edmund Burke 1790

DEDICATION

INTRODUCTION

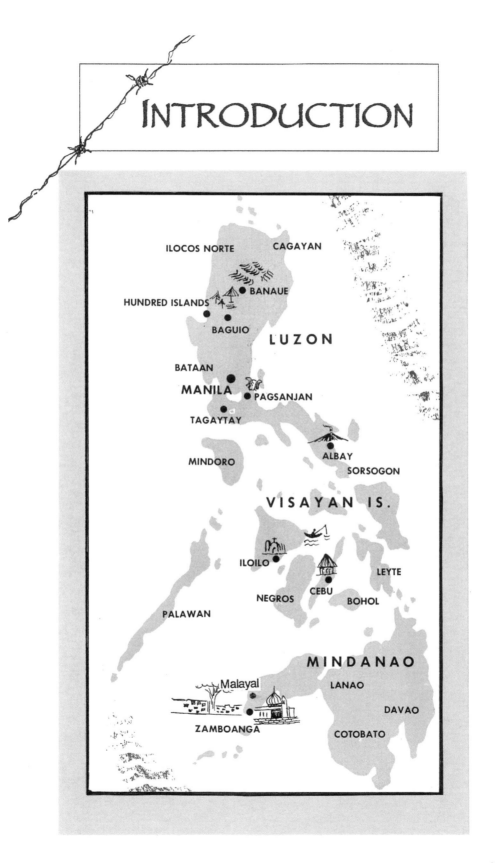

ILOCOS NORTE
CAGAYAN
BANAUE
HUNDRED ISLANDS
BAGUIO
LUZON
BATAAN
MANILA
PAGSANJAN
TAGAYTAY
MINDORO
ALBAY
SORSOGON
VISAYAN IS.
ILOILO
LEYTE
CEBU
NEGROS
BOHOL
PALAWAN
MINDANAO
Malayal
LANAO
DAVAO
ZAMBOANGA
COTOBATO

Introduction

After my arrival in the United States from the Philippines in May of 1945, I was asked to speak at various service organizations, church services, and school groups. Engaging in this exercise enabled me to relive my childhood memories of our family's years spent in that country, as well as the years spent in hiding and as prisoners of the Japanese during World War II. Speaking publicly strongly reinforced my memory, indelibly etching in my mind our family's life before the war. Especially ingrained were the more recent details of the traumatic events, which followed December 8, 1941.

Soon after entering school here, I attempted to write of these experiences. It was good copy. I was not interested in the mundane topic of "What I Did Last Summer," the traditional first-day-of-school assignment. Not having been in school for much of the previous three years left serious gaps in my knowledge of dangling participles and other major errors. My papers came back peppered with red marks and orders to refer to the grammar books. Without any encouragement to continue to record my experiences, I stopped writing.

I did, however, rescue some of the offerings from the waste bin and have included a sampling in this book. I was also able to save entries from two of my diaries, rescued from confiscation, and have inserted these where appropriate.

In addition to my own recollections, I have tapped into the writings of my father and mother: I have included excerpts from these writings to reinforce my memory or to provide supportive information concerning the events that occurred. I have found nothing from them written about the third prison camp we were in, Santo Tomas. I was older then and do have vivid recollections of the events of that time. To lend more graphic description to these events from an adult viewpoint, I have included writings and diary jottings of friends (duly noted), who sent copies of their work either to me or to my parents. In some cases, I have quoted from books written about the period. In general, however, the remembrances of that time are my own.

I leave it to historians, scholars, and military reporters to record troop movements, naval battles, and the politics of that era. Several books written about those years cover the intrigue, secret maneuvering, backbiting, and politicking that was part of the internment life. While affected by all of the above, and certainly aware of some of the goings on, they were not part of my everyday life. I have acquired knowledge of that aspect by reading the memoirs of others.

As a result of being discouraged originally about expressing myself in writing about the era, I entered a long period of silence about the war and seldom spoke of it.

The fiftieth anniversary celebration of our liberation changed all that. Those of us who attended that reunion agreed that it was time to speak out, or to write about that of which few people are aware. What happened in that part of the world to thousands of American, British, and other Allied men, women, and children trapped in the jaws of a rapidly advancing Japanese army as it devoured much of Southeast Asia, is not widely known.

Therefore, what follows is a story of that time as it was lived by the Mattocks family. It is a legacy to my descendants and other interested parties. It is the story of having been caught in the net of the Imperial Japanese Army in its takeover of that part of Asia, and of how we survived.

Now is the time, before my memory fades into oblivion and too many more taps are sounded, to tell you about the extraordinary times in which I grew up.

1 / AN ODYSSEY

ST, STEPHEN'S CHURCH CHOIR, MANILA, C. 1931
DADDY STANDING AT CENTER BACK
MOTHER SEATED AT CENTER FRONT

HENRY MATTOCKS

HENRY

What brought Henry Mattocks and Dorothy Latham halfway around the globe to pursue careers in a land far distant from their roots, and in a milieu neither of them could have envisioned when they set out on their journeys? Lives that began in working class, industrialized cities, watch factories, cotton mills, and coal mines evolved into an odyssey that took them by separate routes to a country that, in most people's minds, existed only in geography books.

In 1917, at age 17, Henry volunteered for service in the British army during the First World War. He served on the Continent and with the Army of Occupation in Cologne, Germany. He had tried to join the navy when he was fourteen, shortly after his brother had been killed in Belgium. The authorities were informed of his actual age, and he was whisked home to Hyde, near Manchester, England, where he began working in the mills as an errand boy. But, having had a taste of life far from the mills and mines, his thirst for adventure had been piqued. He had seen "Paree," so to speak.

The smokestacks and coal mines of northern England, where most of his relatives had been employed for generations, held no appeal for young Henry. From the age of 19 when he returned from the war, his sights were set on emigrating to America. Two aunts who lived nearby owned what was called a sweet shop. Their brother had left for Auburn, Maine years before. Perhaps, if enough money could be saved for passage, part of my father's dream of seeing the world would be realized. Eking out pennies from his job in the mill and help from the aunts in the candy shop made this possible.

He left Liverpool, England in January 1921 and sailed for Portland, Maine where he was met by members of the Wilkinson family, relatives on his mother's side. He lived with them in Auburn until he could find work. Ironically, the only job he could find was in a cotton mill in Lewiston. He moved into housing for the mill workers. Years later, he took us three children to the banks of the Androscoggin River from which stretched row after row of tired, run down, drab, red brick buildings. The cotton industry had since moved South. Pointing up to a third floor window with its shards of glass he said, "That is where I started out!" He lived there for a time in a room with a bare light bulb hanging from the ceiling. He told us of the brawling of the workers in the adjoining rooms as they returned from their Saturday night revelry in the local barrooms.

On Saturday nights Henry tried to get his sleep because Sunday morning, he would attend the early service at the Episcopal Church. In time, the congregation came to know this young Englishman who was so faithful in his attendance. It was at this time that entering the ministry became the focus of his life. Sensing that the Church would be well-served by this man, the Diocese of Maine sponsored his further education at a small school in Monteagle, Tennessee known as DuBose Memorial Church Training School. After two years there he entered Berkeley Divinity School (now a part of Yale University) in Connecticut.

As a seminarian, he spent summers filling in at some interesting places. In the mountains of Tennessee, it took two men to take the service at a little church; one to watch the horses tethered outside so they wouldn't be stolen and one to preach the sermon. Jackman and Newcastle, Maine were Henry's two other summer assignments. He once had a small church in Amarillo, Texas and on Sunday morning rode in with the engineer of the Southern Pacific train to his next parish up the tracks. He had barely a penny to his name and at various times had to pawn what few valuables he possessed.

Decision time came at the end of the three-year seminary program. He knew he wanted missionary work of some type and considered South America. But, just before graduation, Bishop Mosher, the Bishop of the Philippines, spoke about the work there. My father was sold. After being ordained deacon in May of 1929, he accepted the assignment of St. Stephen's Chinese Church in Manila.

He returned to England to visit, and once again bade farewell to his mother and family whom he hadn't seen for eight years. He then set sail for the Orient via the Suez Canal.

While en route on the Indian Ocean, the ship's captain died. There came a call for someone who might be able to conduct a burial service. Henry answered the call and considered the burial rite he performed at sea the first official act of his ministry. It was to figure prominently in his memory because this burial service was a story he told well into his nineties.

In September, shortly after his arrival in Manila, he was ordained priest. After a brief introduction to the work of the church, and a brief introduction to Dorothy Latham, he was dispatched to China to learn the Amoy dialect, the language used by the local Chinese community in the Philippines.

The tales from the China years included one in which he told us that he had to keep a packed suitcase under his desk, ready to grab at a moment's notice as bandits periodically overran the countryside. The owners of the house where he stayed kept dead cats in a tree to ward off evil spirits.

During those days of probing the mysteries of the Chinese word, Henry kept up a correspondence with Dorothy Latham who was teaching at St. Stephen's School in Manila. Midcourse in China, eight months after they had met, on April 7, 1930, Dorothy and Henry were married at St. John's Cathedral in Hong Kong. After a honeymoon in Hong Kong, Dorothy returned to her teaching duties in Manila and Henry continued his studies.

At the end of his year of study, and fluent in the Amoy dialect, Henry returned to Manila to conduct services and church work in his new tongue.

What set him on the road apart from his peers still slogging it out in the pits and mills? He had grown up in a family without a father. While Henry was in the army, his mother had married and eventually had three more sons. A great deal older than this new family, he no longer felt strongly attached to the home he had known, now overseen by a stepfather.

So with the determination to make a life far different from the run of the mill existence around him and having been born with a yen for adventure, he set his sights on distant shores. By dint of perseverance and optimism, and not being discouraged by the twists in the road, he was able to attain his goal.

DOROTHY LATHAM MATTOCKS

S. S. "PRESIDENT PIERCE"
HENRY NELSON, COMMANDER

Distance Run: 391 miles.   2305 miles to Yokohama.

LUNCHEON

Spring Onions   Olives   Indian Relish   Mixed Pickles

Vegetable Soup, Family Style ———— Consomme with Spaghetti

Fried Sanddabs, Colbert Sauce

Salt Codfish Cakes

Veal Cutlets, Breaded with Spaghetti
Mutton Pie, English Style
Scrambled Eggs with Fresh Oysters

(Special) Chicken Chow Mein, Mushrooms

Baked Jacket Potatoes   Beetroot a la Bordelaise

COLD BUFFET
Prime Roast Ribs of Beef Boiled Ham Roast Lamb, Mint Sauce
Liver and Bologne Sausage   Roast Pork   Corned Beef
Roast Chicken   Sardines in Oil

Salad, Celery Root, Mayonnaise
Hearts of Lettuce   Sliced Tomatoes

Vermicelli Custard
Assorted Pastry
Rhubarb Pie   Romien Punch
Boston Doughnuts   Bananas
Fresh Fruits: Apples   Toasted Crackers
Cheese: American Red Rock Tillamook Butter Milk
Tea   Coffee   Cocoa   Fresh Milk

Thursday, January 31st, 1929.

(Afternoon Tea Served in Tea Room at Four o'clock)

A STEAMER passes on the horizon, and
you wonder how far away she is. Visi-
bility at sea varies according to atmos-
pheric conditions, but on clear days
a passing steamer is visible for about
ten miles from the promenade deck.
From the flying bridge, due to its
height, the vessel can be seen
eighteen miles away

DOLLAR STEAMSHIP LINE

MENU

FAREWELL DINNER
TO OUR
SHANGHAI PASSENGERS

S. S. PRESIDENT PIERCE
HENRY NELSON, Commander

DINNER

Captain's Dinner

DOROTHY

Born on June 2, 1900, ten days after Henry's birth on the other side of the Atlantic, Dorothy grew up in the "Watch City" of Waltham, Massachusetts, the youngest of three children. Her father Walter Latham was a watch designer at the Waltham Watch factory, and her mother Mary Fewtrell, is listed in the city records as a mechanic. Both her parents had emigrated from England in the late 1800s.

Unfortunately, Dorothy's mother died in 1903. From then on, a series of housekeepers was employed to care for Dorothy and her siblings. In time, one of the housekeepers, Cora Belle Thomas of Salisbury, Vermont, became her stepmother, and the woman my mother considered "Mother."

Dorothy was a good student. In those days, there were nine years of grammar school before the four of high school; she skipped two grades before high school. In 1917, she graduated valedictorian of her class at Waltham High School. Her valedictory speech reflected her intense interest in the United States' entry into the First World War and world affairs in general. From the Valedictory:

The outlook seems gloomy with all the world at war. We were accused of being luxury-loving, "too proud to fight", and devoid of loyalty and self respect as a people. Despite this apparent darkness, there gleams a splendid manifestation of Americanism. We turn our lawns into gardens, full registration was obtained on draft day...and everybody has bought a Liberty Bond. This awakening of the soul is evident. Growth of national spirit is one great good among others, that so far has come out of so much evil.

After talking about modern inventions such as the wireless and the electric light, she goes on to say:

But now, all these inventions of men's brains, by means of which the world was "getting together", are used for the worst purposes. Now it must be the hearts and souls of nations which shall form a bond of strength.

She went on to matriculate at Boston University, and became the first of her family to graduate from college.

An accomplished musician, she studied piano and later the organ. In her younger days, she was a soprano soloist in various choirs. She was a soloist at her college Baccalaureate in 1921. As a day student at Boston University, she told us that sometimes when the Charles River was frozen, she would skate a part of the way up the river to school. She majored in English, had a flare for languages, and was not afraid of courses such as physics.

From the beginning, she was imbued with a pioneering spirit. She was a founder of the first Girl Scout troop in Waltham. Although her parents were not churchgoers, she joined Christ Church, Waltham, and was baptized at eighteen. From then on, she was active in the activities of that organization. However, despite such lively commitment to local activities, her first job after college graduation was a teaching position at Westford Academy in Westford, Massachusetts.

With a strong interest beyond our shores as demonstrated in her valedictory speech and a commitment to social issues in the community and church, she sought to find a field that would combine these passions. With that in mind, she applied for a position in the mission field. China was her choice. She was told that the China mission quota had been filled, but that in the Philippines there was a considerably large Chinese population. Would she consider going there? She would.

In 1923, at the age of twenty-three, she resigned her position in Westford and said goodbye to her parents, who could not fathom her reason for taking such a major step.

Her many friends went scurrying to their maps. When one said goodbye in those days, it would be at least a month or two before there was an exchange of correspondence. It was to be five years before she saw her parents again.

On the voyage out across the Pacific, the ship stopped at Yokohama. It was the day before the great Yokohama earthquake. My mother went ashore and spent a day getting her first glimpse of life in the Far East. She was fascinated, and was later able to send a few souvenirs she picked up that day back to her parents.

The earthquake struck the next day, September 1. Thankfully, the passengers had returned to the ship that was now well out into the harbor. In a letter dated, September 8, 1923, and written aboard the *SS President Madison* en route to Shanghai, she wrote to a friend:

> The Yokohama earthquake, fire, tidal wave and explosion seem unbelievable. We left there a week ago just as the explosions occurred. The Empress of Australia, a huge Canadian Pacific boat, was already to get underway, when a tidal wave lifted her, stern up, on the dock, smashing her propellers and wrecking some of her machinery....By the way, I went aboard the "Australia" (before the earthquake) since she lay right alongside us....

> It was reported that more than 123,000 people perished that day. (1)

In addition to having had a taste of the exotic wares of Japan, she learned first hand of the destruction that could be wrought in an area plagued with that kind of disaster. For some reason, a Boston paper reported her as missing in the earthquake. Not knowing that she was "missing," Dorothy did not hurry to assure her anxious parents that she was alive and well. A cablegram reporting that all was well was sent from Kobe, the next port of call.

Her assignment in the Philippines: St. Stephen's Chinese Girls' School in Manila. She taught there for a few weeks and then was sent to Amoy, in Fukien province in southern China, to learn the dialect used by the Manila Chinese. The yearlong term was reduced to seven months when she was called back to Manila. However, in that brief time, she managed to become fluent in the Amoy dialect. Also, she had acquired a good knowledge of writing in calligraphy.

At age twenty-five, she became Principal of St. Stephen's School. In 1930, she and Constance Bolderston, another mission teacher, were responsible for founding a junior high component to the school. In addition to her teaching and administrative duties, she played the organ at the church services and directed the choir. The school became coeducational years later, and today it is flourishing with a population of two thousand, five hundred students.

Among the Chinese, she had many friends, both professionally and socially. She was godmother to a host of babies, many of whom kept in touch for years. On her vacations, she took trips to the other islands in the Philippine archipelago, or to Hong Kong, China, or Japan. In late 1928, during her furlough, she took the British freighter, *Malayan Prince* and traveled to Singapore and Egypt eventually ending up in Boston.

Time never hung heavily on her hands. There was never enough of it to do all that she wanted to accomplish, and it could be said that she was years ahead of her time. She never felt hampered in her pursuits by being female, nor was she cowed by anyone. She was very principled, sometimes taking stands that were unpopular, but she held firm. She was frugal; wasting time, electricity, water, food, and paper were cardinal sins. She was not afraid to strike out on her own. All these traits stood her, and us, in good stead in the trials to come in the years ahead.

(1) Joshua Hammer, *Yokohama Burning*, (London: Free Press 2006), p. 243.

2 / HAPPY LIFE

Manila of the Thirties and early Forties was a beautiful city situated by the bay of the same name. Many areas had broad avenues lined with imposing buildings in the Spanish style. Flowers and flowering vines grew in profusion in the gardens of these homes. Large acacia and flame trees lined the boulevards

The beauty of some of the government buildings rivaled those of Washington, DC. Magnificent cathedrals rose above their neighboring buildings. The Walled City, or Intramuros, with its imposing and forbidding Fort Santiago dominated a large part of the area near the Pasig River and waterfront. The streets were crowded with automobiles as well as horse-drawn vehicles called calesas or caromatas. Although there were taxis, buses, and private cars, calesas were the usual mode of transportation.

Like any big city, there were areas where people lived in crowded, run-down houses where the streets were teeming with people, and carts drawn by carabaos (water buffalo) clogged the streets. St. Stephen's School and Church, as well as St. Luke's Hospital, the mission medical center, were in areas that were further from the gracious avenues, which were closer to the waterfront.

The main shopping area was on the Escolta, with department stores like Heacock's and Aguinaldo's, which carried goods from all over the world, even Buster Brown shoes! In contrast, there were, also, open-air markets, which displayed the fruits, vegetables, and meats brought in from the provinces. Local handicrafts were available at tiny tiendas (stores) and sari sari stores (convenience stores, carrying a bit of everything), which lined the side streets. Vendors, selling snacks of fried bananas, bucayo (coconut candy), rice balls, and balut (embryonic duck eggs) hawked their wares along with everyone else. Australian butter, beef, and lamb were available in grocery stores.

At the time, there was a cosmopolitan feel to the city. In

addition to the Filipinos and the Chinese, the population was comprised of people from many nations. During the Great Depression, in the Thirties, Americans moved there for employment opportunities. The country needed engineers to build roads and railroads, teachers for the schools, medical personnel for the clinics, geologists for the mining industry as well as businessmen to represent some of the major corporations and banks of the world. Missionaries established schools and religious and medical centers. Veterans from the Spanish-American War had married Filipinas and remained in the Islands. Europeans, as well as people from other parts of Asia, became part of the lively mixture of races and nationalities.

So it was in this vibrant tropical city that Dorothy and Henry settled down to their chosen work; she to continue her involvement in the school she had been involved with since the early Twenties, and he to begin parish work at St. Stephen's Chinese School and Church.

After Henry's return from China, the couple settled into a house on Calle Valenzuela in the Santa Mesa section of Manila. A few months after moving in, I was born.

Because of their close ties with the Chinese community, I was baptized with a Chinese name in addition to my English one. My godparents were both Chinese and American. My Chinese name is Ma Beng Tsu, which translated means "horse, clear pearl." The Ma is for the "M" and "A", the first two letters of Mattocks, and Tsu, meaning pearl, is for Margaret, my first name. Clear Jade and Clear Wisdom were the Chinese names given to my sister and brother, respectively. Like me, they also had Chinese and American godparents.

I was told that my first word was "oozo" meaning "lizard," not a common first word! This was because the ceiling of the house was covered with little lizards which sometimes flopped down into the crib.

Santa Mesa in those days was somewhat rural; therefore, we were able to have ducks and chickens as well as two dogs called Terry and Toota. Mother went back to the school soon after I was born. My first amah (nursemaid), Jeofela, cared for me. Later, Carolina appeared on the scene. I treasure today an embroidered pillowcase she stitched for me.

Two years after the Santa Mesa move, my sister Shirley was born. Santa Mesa was home until 1934 when my parents were due for a furlough. The house was closed up, and we sailed for England across the Pacific and via Canada. I marvel now to think about how Mother managed on the ships, trains, buses, taxis, subways, and rickshaws with me, almost three years old, and Shirley, nearly one. There weren't any of the conveniences of traveling with small children that there are available today. My grandfather met the train in Montreal and, for the first time, met his son-in-law and his granddaughters. He had not seen his daughter for five years. Following this brief introduction, we boarded a ship and sailed across the Atlantic to meet the other half of the family in England.

In England, Shirley and I stayed with our grandmother while our parents toured the country. The rest of the furlough was spent in Waltham, Massachusetts with our Latham grandparents. In late 1934, my father returned to Manila alone, and we followed a few months later.

Upon our return we were assigned to a mission residence at 606 Taft Avenue, an impressive Spanish-style structure in an area of stately homes. It was constructed of stucco, and ornate wrought iron grillwork graced its windows. The University of the Philippines was across the street. The house had been a Roman Catholic orphanage known as the House of the Holy Child until it was bought for Episcopal mission use.

The Mattocks family occupied the second floor, while the first floor was assigned to the Harveys, a family of three. Benson Harvey was the canon missioner of the diocese, and, in that capacity, was away a good deal of the time visiting mission stations in other parts of the islands. Additionally, a small apartment was the domain of Elizabeth Gordon Griffin, the mission treasurer. We children were fascinated with Miss Griffin, for she carried a huge pocketbook with her initials EGG (without periods) emblazoned on the front. We used to giggle and call her "Egg." Coincidentally, she always had a wonderful Easter egg hunt for us in her apartment. Maybe she was having the last laugh.

Because Mother had not had time to supervise the cleaning of the orphanage before our arrival and the impending arrival of the new baby, it was in a rather sorry state in terms of cleanliness. Perhaps because of this, I contracted bacillary dysentery and had to be hospitalized for quite a while. I was in St. Luke's, our mission hospital, where I had been born four years earlier. My father slept on a cot in the corner of the open-air room during my illness. I had to learn to walk again and due to the high fever, my hair fell out. While there, I came down with the measles. Since contagious cases were not permitted at St. Luke's, I was sent home to recuperate. A long recovery followed. The hospitalization and subsequent recuperative period remains vivid in my memory,

Since "606" was designed for institutional use, a great hallway extended from one end of the building to the other, and down one side several dormitory-like rooms opened up onto this hall. On the other side was a huge sala (living room) and dining room that opened up onto a large porch enclosed with fancy grillwork. One bathroom served the whole floor, and it, too, was outfitted for dormitory use. To provide one with an idea of the extent of the hallway, I learned to ride a two-wheeled bicycle up and down its length. Shirley and I shared a room at the family end of the corridor, and my parents and Geoffrey, who was born shortly after we moved into the house, shared the room next to us.

The property was surrounded on three sides by a seven-foot high stone wall, which was embedded with shards of glass along the top, a deterrent to would-be intruders. The yard was spacious and shaded by huge acacia trees. A little nipa (palm frond) playhouse provided us with many hours of fun. Sometimes Shirley and I put Geoffrey in a little rattan baby carriage and pushed him around the yard. The lavandera (wash lady) did the laundry at a rectangular cement enclosure next to the house. We changed our clothes often in the hot, sticky weather. She would also do the ironing using a heavy iron made of cast iron that was filled with hot coals. Everything was starched and crisp. In those days, men wore white suits, which crumpled easily in the heat. Many of our dresses were hand-smocked. Some were made of cotton, and others were sewn from a delicate fabric called piña, a material made from the pineapple plant.

The three of us were carefully watched over by Serafina, our amah. We were not allowed out alone anywhere. I can still almost feel her tight grip around my wrist as she took us out for walks in the neighborhood. She and her husband Pedro Olivarez who was called "Oliver" by Mother, lived at the other end of the hall from our family quarters. Oliver did the marketing and the cooking. They had come to work in our house separately. In time, however, they married. In due course Bernard was born, followed by Elizabeth whom we called "Betsy." We children enjoyed playing with them and pushing them around the property in the little wicker baby carriage, which by then, Geoffrey had outgrown.

In addition to the Olivarez family, there was Catalino, the gardener, who tended the profusion of flowers that grew on the premises. Dark purple bougainvillea climbed the walls, and the fragrance from the beautiful little sampaguitas filled the air. Colorful calla lilies grew in cultivated beds, and the delicate frangipani provided additional color and fragrance. Catalino doubled as a chauffeur. Mother had driven the Model A Ford, but had had an unfortunate accident with a filled-to-the-top garbage truck; this left her skittish about driving, so Catalino navigated the streets after that. Then there was Antonio, the houseboy. Each day he polished the cement floors by using coconut husks. Antonio would stand barefoot, one foot on each husk, and sashay around the floors giving them a brilliant shine.

Our home also did duty as the mission guesthouse. Refugees from all over the Far East, guests of the mission passing through, and priests awaiting assignments were all part of the family, temporarily. Visitors occupied the several spare bedrooms along the long hallway most of the time. Mother planned the meals, but since she was involved with teaching, meal preparation and child care were the province of the Olivarezes. I don't remember a time when we dined as a family of five. We children ate by ourselves on the porch adjoining the kitchen. Many years later, Serafina, refreshing my memory about the days at Taft Avenue, reminded me that I was a fussy eater. Eating apart from my parents was probably a good thing because Serafina was quite lenient and gave in to my whims.

I could never learn to like or drink the canned evaporated milk, which was a staple of our diet. Many a potted palm got a "watering" of milk from me when no one was looking. There was a dairy in Manila called, "Magnolia," which sold cold fresh milk in bottles and also a little ice cream treat called "Tidbits." We'd hear the tinkle of the bell as the Magnolia milk truck plied the streets. But that was as near as we got to replacing the canned milk.

We really enjoyed the delicious fruits: papayas served with the juice of the calamanci, mangoes, lanzones, and chicos. *Masarap!* (Delicious) Vegetables were plentiful as well, and eggplant, pechay (a kind of cabbage), and camotes (sweet potatoes) were often served.

The adults dined at a late hour and in somewhat formal style. We children were usually in bed by serving time although we were allowed to greet the guests. On a couple of occasions, Shirley and I sneaked out of bed and down the hall to just outside the dining room to listen to the grown-up conversations. That is when I first heard the mission refugees who had just escaped from Nanking, China talk about the atrocities there. I was six years old, and I didn't want to hear any more.

The first night the Nanking missionaries stayed with us, they all had their watches stolen from under their pillows where they had been told they would be safe. The next morning, the police were at the house surveying the greasy footprints that led across the kitchen floor out to the porch. A few months earlier, Shirley and I had had our pink Mickey Mouse piggy banks stolen right from under our noses. I lay in bed under the mosquito net and watched the dark figure of a man reach out and snatch the banks. It was a while before I dared call out to my parents. By that time, the intruder was gone. After several more such robberies, a watchman was hired to guard the property at night.

When our amahs wanted us to obey, they told us that the "bombay" would get us if we didn't mind them. Many Indian Sikhs were hired as watchmen and guards throughout the city and were called "bombays." Needless to say, we steered clear of any bombays we saw. When my parents needed protection from the rash of breaking and entering, they sought the services of a bombay. Of course, with our friendly private bombay, we children soon felt that the amahs' threats had lost their punch.

When I was four, my mother started me, and subsequently the others, on the Calvert School Home Study system. Books and lesson plans were sent from the Calvert headquarters in Baltimore, Maryland. Many children whose parents were posted to the far corners of the world studied under this system. Periodically our work would be sent back to headquarters for appraisal and comparison with our stateside peers. It was not an average curriculum. Since many of the families traveled extensively, there was a great deal of emphasis on geography and history. There was a fine arts unit with art plates that we learned much from, the way kids today pore over baseball cards. When on furlough in 1939, I entered a third grade class for three months. I had no problem whatsoever, even though it was my first experience in a traditional classroom, and my previous "school" experience had been sporadic at best.

In addition to the Calvert studies, Mrs. Huang came to tutor us in Chinese. We were entranced with her bound feet and the intricately embroidered slippers which encased them. Miss Ancell came to do arithmetic. Our school hours were somewhat hit or miss because Mother continued to teach at St. Stephen's. For a time Audrey, the daughter of friends, came to the house to join me in the classes.

We were taken to the Manila Symphony, and we had swimming lessons at the YMCA. I studied piano at the Academy of Music, which was run by the Lobregat sisters, a formidable pair. In order to have proper hand placement over the keys, a peseta (20 centavo piece) was placed on each wrist. If the peseta fell off, a rap on the wrist would make certain it didn't happen again. There was talk of a room with mice if a student showed a lack of practice. Luckily, I never knew if this was true. There was interminable rhythm practice with drumsticks. There were some grand recitals, full blown affairs at San Beda Hall, an auditorium that seated five or six hundred people. In addition to the recital piece, the children were involved in tableaux involving singing and rhythmical movements. I was kept on my toes as my parents always sat in the front row.

Shirley and I had a bit of an enterprise going. We put together a little "newspaper." We called the project "Blue Hats." We got our name from the hats of the students who exited the University of the Philippines across the street. They must have been in an ROTC program because they all wore military style blue caps. It was a record of our daily events that we noted and illustrated. Anyway, we made a few centavos from our venture.

St. Stephen's Chinese Church was a calesa ride across the Pasig River. Mother was the organist and choir director. My father conducted the services, including the sermon, in Chinese. I sat on the left side of the church with all the females; the men and boys were on the right. One Sunday when the Bishop was preaching, I got away from my amah and tore up the center aisle with the book that was given to me to keep me occupied. I asked the Bishop to read from it because it was more interesting than what he was saying. From then on, I was packed off to the English-speaking Cathedral of St. Mary and St. John for Sunday School.

I must have been better behaved there because the selfsame Bishop and his wife invited me to their very formal Sunday dinners at "Bishopstead" on a number of occasions. I knew I had to eat everything that was served. It is funny what sticks in one's mind; the Bishop used a huge pepper mill and with a grand flourish peppered everything on his plate.

Early in my father's experience preaching at St. Stephen's, there occurred, during a Sunday service, a huge ruckus at the back of the church. A man had entered the building, tripped over a capiz shell screen that blocked the street noise, and had fallen flat on his face—prostrate down in the center aisle. No one in the pews budged. So Daddy came down from the chancel to help the man. He was restrained by several parishioners from doing so. The reason: if the man were dead and my father touched him, he would be responsible for paying for the funeral.

Typhoons and earthquakes were part of the experience. Once, when our parents were having dinner, a huge rattling and shaking began. Earthquake! The pudding that had just been served, flipped over. Geoffrey's crib, which was on rollers, began to roll down the long hallway. Just as it was about to tumble down the grand cement staircase, one of the guests cornered it. We all rushed outside. The several-storied apartment building next door swung back and forth like the pendulum of a clock. Typhoons brought flooding. In the aftermath of one particularly strong one, small boats were used to navigate the streets.

We played with friends from several districts in the city. Sometimes we went to the beach at Cavite; other times to the

Army-Navy Club. A Sunday picnic to Tagaytay was a favorite outing. From the Tagaytay ridge, we could see an active volcano rising from the midst of Lake Taal; a spectacular view that kept us mesmerized.

It was always a gala event when we went down to Pier 7 to greet incoming liners bringing friends or to say farewell to those departing. Leaving and departing, in retrospect, was a rather leisurely and unhurried event, with bands, flowers, on-board refreshments, and, just before departure, colorful streamers unfurling from the ship as it slowly left the pier. When it was time for visitors to disembark, a white-coated crew member would travel the decks playing on a gong, announcing the imminent departure of the ship. Mother always lingered with her bon voyage wishes and made her way to the gangplank just as it was being separated from the ship's side. This made us all very nervous. Those passengers on the ship who were bound for the United States would be on board for several weeks. Most likely the ship would make calls at the ports of Hong Kong, Shanghai, Nagasaki, Kobe, Yokohama, and Honolulu.

Another event that drew people to the piers at the bay was the arrival of the *China Clipper*, a seaplane, which brought a few passengers and mail from the States. In the late Thirties, with the advent of *Clipper* service, mail from America arrived in a matter of days rather than months.

When school was out, our family took its vacation north of Manila up in Baguio, a pleasantly cool city in the Mountain Province. We piled in the Model A with Catalino, our chauffeur, and made our way up the Zig Zag Trail. We were always excited by the first whiff of the smell of the pine trees. The Zig Zag Trail was a torturous two-lane road with twists and turns and steep precipices on either side. A cottage on the grounds of Brent School was provided for our stay. Sometimes the air was cool enough for a sweater and a fire, a welcomed respite from the sweltering heat in Manila. In Baguio, our mission supported Easter School where the Igorot students studied as well as learned to weave beautiful fabrics of vibrant hues. We enjoyed pony rides in Burnham Park and were entranced by the downtown market. Because of the mountain climate, even strawberries grew. The showy orange and yellow blossoms of the nasturtium plant spilled over into gardens and onto walls and fences. Bouquets of colorful straw-like flowers we called "everlasting" were offered for sale in the marketplace. We took some of these back to Manila with us, a reminder of our sojourn in the mountains.

In May of 1939, it was our turn for furlough. We boarded the *Empress of Japan* and steamed out of Manila Bay for Vancouver, Canada. In what turned out to be his last letter to Mother, Grandpa Latham wrote:

Hoping that you have a good trip and do not meet any Japanese or German submarines, or any other fool thing that the wise men of this world are making to destroy themselves and others with.

In the same letter, he expresses a bit of concern for our nomadic lifestyle. In reference to the time we are to spend with them, he says:

It seems good to us for the children to have as much time in one place as your work will allow, but in spite of their roaming lives, they seem to thrive and develop very well.

Our arrival in Vancouver coincided with a state visit of King George VI and Queen Elizabeth of England. We joined the waving onlookers at the sidewalk.

After a visit with friends in Seattle, we crossed the United States by train. The three of us were looking forward to seeing our grandparents. For Geoffrey, it would be an introduction. Our grandfather was building us a playhouse in the backyard. Some of the lumber had come from the wreckage of the hurricane of 1938. We had received letters from Grandpa before our departure from Manila describing the progress of the building project, and we were filled with anticipation.

Mother's brothers met us at the train in Newtonville, Massachusetts; and it was there that she was given the news that her father had died on her birthday, June 2, just after we had arrived in British Columbia. Our first function on arrival, then, was to attend my grandfather's funeral. I have to admit that after months of looking forward to seeing him, I was somewhat dismayed by the appearance of the copper urn containing his ashes, which sat on the front seat of the car on our way to the cemetery. For an eight-year old, it took a little adjustment.

My parents, after a short rest, spent the furlough speaking at various churches and organizations. Shirley and I were taken to the New York World's Fair. Fascination with the Automat (forerunner of the vending machine), the Lady with No Head, and the Woman Buried in a Cake of Ice, fair sideshow attractions, were what we talked about for days; much to my parents' chagrin, I suspect.

We children got used to the idea of being in a neighborhood and having friends appear on the doorstep. I was sent alone on errands three and four blocks away to pick up groceries. Until then, I had never been out of the yard on my own. We did ask our grandmother, however, who was introducing us to fresh peaches, to please serve the kind that grew in the Philippines instead. Canned!

Toward the end of our stay, my father received word that his next assignment upon return to the Philippines, was to be Zamboanga, Mindanao in the southern islands.

MOVE TO MINDANAO

As children, we were a little apprehensive about the move to Mindanao.

During the furlough, we had intended to visit the relatives in England; but, with the war in Europe, it was decided that it would be better for the family not to go. So at Christmastime 1939, my father went alone to see his mother and other relatives. On the return trip, sailing out of Glasgow, his ship was attacked and was forced to return to the port. The damage was not serious, and he was able to depart in a couple of days. As it happened, this visit with his mother turned out to be his last.

Because of the war, we had been loath to get on a liner and cross the Atlantic. However, the rumors and rumblings of a conflict in the Far East did not stop us from gathering up our bags, boarding the *Empress of Asia* in Vancouver, and setting sail across the Pacific at the end of January 1940.

The ship, in total blackout, zigzagged her way across the ocean to Manila. At stops at Yokohama and Nagasaki, we could see the difference on the docks from the months before. Our cameras were confiscated when we went ashore. The cultured-pearl vendors were not at their usual posts on the docks. At a visit to one of the missions, the people told us in whispered tones of the preparations for war and pointed out grassy mounds in the garden where they said that guns and ammunition were buried.

The Yangtze River at Shanghai was filled with both sampans and Japanese warships. We children stood on the deck of our ship staring at the khaki-clad Japanese soldiers lining the railings of the anchored destroyers. The sight of so many warships filled with uniformed troops was a curiosity, and it brought a little excitement into the routine of shipboard life. It would be only a matter of months before those same warships and soldiers would be steaming southward in their effort to conquer Southeast Asia.

Shortly after we left Shanghai, a terrible typhoon arose. The ship creaked and groaned as it sank into the troughs of water created by the parting waves. In a moment it would be riding the crest of the monster waves, its bow well out of the water, only to plunge downward again into the churning chasms of the angry ocean. Huge waves swept over even the highest decks. Looking through our cabin porthole, we saw only swirling water pounding against the sides of the ship. At night, the shuddering and shaking of the ship kept us awake and alert. Our life preservers were never far from us. We were good sailors, but most of the passengers were overcome with violent seasickness. To our great relief, the storm abated after two or three days, and we experienced much smoother sailing.

Hong Kong was the last stop before Manila. Going ashore here was fun for the children. We looked forward to the ride on the tramway up Victoria Peak as well as the ride on the Star Ferry across the harbor crowded with junks. A bus ride took us to the Stanley market and the area where our parents had spent their honeymoon.

Shortly after our arrival in Manila, Daddy went ahead to his new assignment in Zamboanga. Mother and we children stayed temporarily in Manila in the Nurses' Home at St. Luke's

Hospital while arrangements were made for our things to be shipped south. Already, the house on Taft Avenue had new residents. After two months, we said goodbye to the city we had considered home and headed for Mindanao on the inter-island steamer, the *Don Esteban.*

3 ZAMBOANGA

While we were still in Manila, Daddy wrote to his brothers in England:

ST. JOHN'S CHINESE SCHOOL
ZAMBOANGA, PHILIPPINES

聖　公　會
菲律濱三寶顏聖約翰學校

DOROTHY L. MATTOCKS · PRINCIPAL
REV. H. T. BURKE · BURSAR
MR. PAUL T. K. CHOU · SUPERVISOR

P. O. Box No. 157

May 1st, 1940

校長　馬顯理
司庫　麥亨利
主任　周登恩
信箱第一五七號

Just a line to say that I am getting more settled now in this bungalow by the sea, although Dorothy and the children have not yet come from Manila. It is a lovely place with beautiful sunsets and I shall be glad when the rest of the family gets here to enjoy it. Well, I am at the other end of the world now and I have never seen a lovelier place. Every night I can hear the waves pounding against my front garden wall,—and Europe seems so very far away, but I am thinking of you all. I get the news every day from the United States Army barracks here. Just two typewritten sheets......

After a three-day sail from Manila, having stopped at Cebu and Iloilo, we docked at the pantalan (pier) in Zamboanga. As the ship docked, swarms of little bancas (outriggered boats) came alongside. Little boys called up to the passengers on the deck to toss coins over the side. The passengers complied, and soon the waters were filled with boys jumping off the bancas and diving for the money that was rapidly sinking to the bottom of the sea. Daddy met the ship, and we were driven in a calesa to 114 Cawa Cawa, our "bungalow by the sea."

Zamboanga City sits at the tip of a peninsula in the province of Zamboanga on the island of Mindanao, the second largest island in the Philippine archipelago. It was a romantic spot known as the "City of Flowers." The fragrance of frangipani; bougainvillea; hibiscus; and sampaguita, the national flower, filled the air. Orchids of varied colors hung from balconies.

The city bordered the Sulu Sea, and ships plying the waters to the Dutch East Indies would call at the port. Shortly after our arrival, Japanese ships passed through, loaded with scrap iron and metal of all sorts to be used in the munitions factories in Japan.

At one end of the downtown area, a formidable fortress, Fort Pilar, dominated the scene overlooking the sea. On its grounds stood Pettit Barracks, the outpost of a United States Army garrison. At the other end of the main road leading along the waterfront was a Moro (local Islamic tribe) fishing village built out over the water and accessible by a framework of "ladders" laid parallel to the water.

Small parks and fountains dotted the downtown area. The Plaza Hotel was the center of much of the social life. The Cine Ideal featured American films including "Snow White and the Seven Dwarfs," my first movie. The OK Bazaar carried everything from roller skates to fabrics. Mrs. Cooley's Curio Shop was a place of fascination for a child. She had a wonderful display of local handicrafts that we never tired of eyeing. Upstairs a talented seamstress embroidered the beautiful dresses we wore.

Impressive statues, including one of the Philippine national hero, Jose Rizal, occupied prominent places in the plazas. The pace of life in this southern city was more relaxed than in Manila.

Near the center of town was an open-air market filled with an abundant display of fruits and vegetables. At one end, flies swarmed around the carcasses of freshly slaughtered pigs, steer, and chickens hanging from bamboo poles. Women, whose teeth were worn to stubs by chewing betel nut, called out as one passed by. There were tubs of squirming fish. Moros in colorful dress squatted beside their crafts of wood carvings, brass work, and weavings. A trip to the market was an everyday occurrence for the cooks of the house.

It was difficult to look at the carcasses of the slaughtered pigs. Everyday several ox-drawn carts, whipped into a furious canter, clattered along the road by our house. The drivers urged the oxen on with whips and blood-curdling yells. In the carts were squealing pigs on their way to the slaughterhouse. The pigs bounced around, squealing and tumbling all over themselves. Like clockwork during siesta, the carts thundered by. A few hours later, the wagons returned at a much slower pace with the remains of the pigs piled in a heap in the back. It made a tremendous impression on me; and, for a long time, I had a hard time eating pork.

Cawa Cawa Street stretched out to the north along the shore. Past the Philippine Constabulary Barracks and an open field were three identical red and white bungalows facing the sea. Ours was the first of these. Just past the bungalows was the house of the mission doctor, Dr. Trota and his family. The mission compound, which included Brent Hospital, St. Alban's School (formerly The Moro Settlement School), and St. John's Chinese School, where Mother was the principal, completed the neighborhood.

The house at Cawa Cawa was built high off the ground with wooden latticework enclosing the ground level. A spacious front porch with capiz shell sliders looked out across the sea. Off the back porch was the kitchen with its huge kerosene stove. Several times a week, ice from Mr. Wilson's ice plant was delivered. We had no telephone, no refrigerator, no car, and, at first, no radio. Despite the lack of modern conveniences, we soon felt at home in this "lovely place by the sea."

We shared the house with our amah and household help, Angracia, Jeofela, and Juliana. Next door lived a Spanish family with five beautiful daughters. Local Filipino and Mestizo swains would sit on the seawall outside their house playing their guitars and serenading the girls with love songs nightly. No one ever appeared at the windows to give them encouragement, but that did not dampen their ardor. Mother, to no avail, in the wee hours, would yell out the window and ask them to move on.

We quickly made friends with some of the children of the teachers of the school. The Enriquez children, Edna and twins Joy and Jewel, were frequent visitors. Remy, the daughter of the Dr. and Mrs. Trota, was a constant companion. To this day, we reminisce about the days we spent together playing games the local children enjoyed. Sometimes we invented our own. We sang songs we had been taught such as, "Planting Rice" and "My Nipa Hut is Very Small." One of the popular songs of the day was entitled "Don't You Go, to Far Zamboanga!"

There was another mission group, the Christian and Missionary Alliance (C&MA), stationed outside the city at Tetuan. This group was to have great importance in our lives when we fled from the city to the mountains in the early days of the war. Previous to that, we children visited their compound on occasion. They adhered to fairly strict Biblical rules of conduct in their daily lives, while we were bound by a much freer interpretation. There was no card playing or playing with dolls on Sunday! Arlene, one of the oldest children of the Tetuan mission and I, having shared living in Zamboanga, hiding in the mountains, being together in prison camps and on prison ships remain the fastest of friends. We still recount some of the simple ways we managed to have fun despite the conditions under which we found ourselves.

Being treated to evening displays of glorious tropical sunsets with vibrant reds, oranges, and yellows splashed across the horizon was a panorama we relished. Close to the equator, darkness came very quickly. After the sun had slipped below the horizon, the planet Venus made its appearance. It cast a brilliant, shimmering streamer of light across the waters. After the war came and we were imprisoned, I sometimes looked up into the sky at the moon, the stars, and planets. I thought about how people who were free would be gazing at the same heavens and how long it might be before we would be free again, if ever.

After darkness had descended, the Moro fishermen would wade waist-deep out into the waters carrying a flaming torch in one hand and a spear in the other. By day, they sailed colorful vintas. These were small outriggered boats propelled by magnificent rectangular sails resembling multicolored patchwork quilts. No two were the same. Some of the families who made their living by the sea lived on these boats, the only shelter from the sun and rain being a small nipa (palm frond) roof over the midsection of the vinta.

Not far out into the sea were two long slender slivers of islands, fringed with coconut trees: Big and Little Santa Cruz. Their sands were a lovely pink, made so by the crushed coral. We enjoyed picnics and shell gathering expeditions on their shores. Excerpts from a composition I wrote in Santo Tomas Internment Camp describes a surprise outing to these islands.

Adrift on a Vinta

The hot sun shone on the blue sea and the little waves rippled into the shore teasing the sand and beckoning someone to play with them. We accepted this call. Two nurses from the hospital; two attendants; Remy, my girlfriend; my sister; and I decided to go for a sail in the hospital vinta...the sail of our vinta was one of the most picturesque of the busy port.

Before we left, Mother warned us that dinner would soon be ready, so stay close to the shore. The bay was full of swift and dangerous currents. My, it was hot! We had no protection from the sun. We did not realize the danger we were in, until we found ourselves bumping into Little Santa Cruz. Santa Cruz was widely known for its rare and beautiful shells. We all clambered ashore, determined to make the best of it and to, at least, have something to show for our unexpected voyage.

After gathering a considerable number of shells, we climbed back into the vinta and unfurled the sail. However, a gale had come up and we found ourselves being carried further out to sea. The boys took the sail down and we just drifted until we hit a current. Fortunately, the force of the current carried us many kilometers across the sea to the mainland to Taluksangay, a fishing village a few kilometers up the east coast of the peninsula . At one spot a huge monkey came leaping out toward us, jumping from rock to rock.

We had the monkey coming for us on one side and a large white launch bearing down on us on the other. On the back of the launch, a man was frantically waving a pair of dungarees.

Much to our surprise we found the occupants of the launch to be our parents, who tried not to be angry, but were aghast at our lobster-red skin. The vinta was hitched up to the launch and we speedily made our way to the pantalan. The fleet was in, and our unexpected arrival amused the sailors immensely. Sunburned, tired, and hungry we took a calesa home after a dangerous, but exciting escapade.

◆

As in Manila, Shirley and I studied under Mother's tutelage with the Calvert School system. We did not have the outside tutors here so we were left on the honor system a great deal of the time to do the work laid out for us. I know that we took quite a few recesses and went over the sea wall to the beach when we probably should have been more diligent about our studies. We had a signal worked out. As soon as we saw the girls in their pink uniforms from the Pilar Institute up the road coming out for lunch, it was time to head indoors. Geoffrey had more of a routine, since he attended kindergarten at the Moro Settlement School.

The afternoons weren't as free for me as the mornings. Mother enrolled me in St. John's Chinese School where she was the principal. Their afternoon classes were conducted in Chinese. A piece I wrote many years ago describes the experience.

Attendance at Chinese School

My attendance at Chinese School was not marked by achievement. I was the only white student in the school. I stood with the others when we began class by standing and paying respects to Dr. Sun Yat-sen, whose portrait hung on the classroom wall.

However, when the students were called to the board, they made a point of stroking my blonde hair as they passed by. Others ran their fingers up my arm to test the authenticity of my skin. I was not offended by this. As a matter of fact, I remember basking in the attention, figuring that this was the way I was going to get by since I really didn't know what was going on in the classroom in an academic way.

The teacher spoke in the Amoy dialect to teach the Mandarin language. To my ears, it all sounded the same. When on rare occasions, I attempted to speak, I combined the two tongues. This brought gales of laughter (good-natured, I was told later) from my classmates and my resolve to keep my mouth shut.

I did better at copying the characters that we did by the hour. I liked mixing the ink stick with the water on the ink stone and using my brush to painstakingly retrace the characters in my copybook. At least I was on equal footing doing this exercise.

Although I came to understand Chinese, I seldom spoke it. It was a bright moment when there was a realization that I did understand, and my parents could no longer lapse into the language in my presence when they wanted confidentiality.

♦

Now, I like to think that this school experience gave me a bit of empathy for the feelings of my students during my tenure as a bilingual teacher years later.

Many of the people in Zamboanga spoke a dialect known as Chabacano, sort of a pidgin Spanish. I managed to learn a little of this and was able to communicate with some of my friends.

Besides her duties at the school, Mother was organist at Holy Trinity Church where Daddy was the Priest-In-Charge. Trinity was located at the other end of town outside Pettit Barracks. Geoffrey, although only five or six, used to take his turn pumping the organ by a rather large handle on the side. The congregation was an assorted one: army personnel, mission staff, local Westerners, Filipinos, and Chinese. Despite my father's proficiency in Chinese and having been sent to Zamboanga at the request of the local Chinese, he conducted the services in English because of the mixed nature of the congregation. However, there was ample opportunity to use Chinese at the school.

On Sunday mornings, we took a calesa to church. More than once, our trip was held up by the antics of one of our monkeys who chose this moment to escape from his cage when everyone was rushing around. Amfalula was a crafty creature. He knew how to create a scene just when it mattered most. Just as the calesa was drawing up in front of the house, this monkey would somehow unlatch his cage and take to the rafters above the kitchen, jumping from one to another.

After trying all sorts of coaxing and cajoling to get him down, Mother hit on a brilliant idea. Sticky flypaper came in large sheets. She put one of the sheets on the kitchen table and placed a banana in the middle. Amfalula, spying the fruit, made a great leap onto the table and was at once trapped! All four paws and tail were firmly glued to the paper. From then on we got to the church on time.

In addition to Amfalula, we had a little monkey, Dinky; a cat, Coreopsis; and two dogs. I am not sure how we acquired it, but, at one time, there was a baby crocodile that lived in our outside washing enclosure. We tried to feed it all sorts of food, from bread to fish. But this reptile went on a hunger strike and soon died.

Our pleasures were simple. Pasonanca was an attractive park not far from the city. Situated on its grounds was a lovely natural swimming pool surrounded by rocks, ferns, gorgeous orchids, and flowers. The water was cool and pristine. On the grounds was a magnificent tree house. How we looked forward to a trip up there on the open air local bus! Swimming in the waters of the Sulu Sea right at our doorstep was a daily ritual.

It was always exciting when the huge Sears Roebuck catalog arrived in the mail. We were miles from the department stores in Manila. Shirley and I pored over its pages for hours imagining how we would furnish our make-believe "plantation." We entertained ourselves at length listing the families on the "plantation," planning the social life of the children, and choosing from the catalog the toys and clothes we would buy for them. This fantasy play was not engaged in because of a feeling of deprivation, but was an imaginative sort of activity we developed in our free time.

The only social life that I remember my parents participating in, apart from a few dinners or an occasional movie, was a Monday evening event at the Army Navy Club. The children's menu at home was always the same on Monday night: a fish called lapu-lapu or one called tanguingue, rice and peas, and, of course, evaporated milk. The milk was easy, as a potted palm stood nearby, but the fish took a bit of doing and help from the dogs and cat. Years later, I tried those fish again and thought they were delicious; in the prison camps I looked back on the Monday night menu with nostalgia.

After dinner, Shirley and I frequently wanted to go to Trotas to play. Our amahs were fearful about letting us out along the seawall after dark, as well they should have been. A couple of times we managed to "sneak" out after we plied them with American magazines that we kept aside for this purpose. Dr. and Mrs. Trota did not support our adventures and soon accompanied us home. We must have paid Geoffrey off in some way, for I don't recall that he was part of the scheme. It was years before I told mother about these after-dark "escapes." She was incredulous.

I had piano lessons from a local teacher and did enjoy playing. Shirley had violin lessons from a woman who came over from Basilan Island. She and her family were plantation owners; and when there was business in Zamboanga City, she included a violin lesson. After we were in bed at night, Mother and she would play duets. The haunting second movement of Mendelsohn's Violin Concerto in E minor was a favorite. To this day, when I hear that particular movement, I am taken back to the sad notes drifting across the room with the background of the pounding surf, all the sadder because the whole plantation family was annihilated during the invasion.

There were many fiestas in town for all sorts of reasons, but the religious feast days were celebrated in grand fashion with parades, music, food, paper lanterns, and banners bearing the likeness of the particular saint being honored. We did not attend the festivities in the plaza because we were fearful of the juramentados. A juramentado (meaning "oath taker") was a Muslim who believed he would go to heaven on a white horse if he killed a Christian or Christians. He expected that in the end, he would be killed as well. There was a ritual associated with this suicide mission. In preparation, the juramentado would bind himself in white and arm himself with a kris (long sword). His identity would not be known to the assembled, but only to the Sultan. A priest then had a hand in preparing the juramentado for the suicide mission. Fiestas celebrating Christian feast days were times when the possibility of a juramentado strike would be greatest. When an attack began, cries of "juramentado!" would go up from the scattering crowd.

A story was told that one of the mission hospital orderlies kept one at bay by pointing his wooden parade rifle at the attacker. No one in our family ever witnessed a juramentado attack, but we certainly were frightened at the prospect. Despite this, at times other than feast days, we felt safe going into town by ourselves, swimming in the ocean, or riding our bicycles along the sea wall.

When school was out, we sometimes took a trip on an inter-island steamer either to Manila or another island. On one such trip, Mother and I went to Jolo, an island in the Sulu Archipelago. The Moros there had a reputation for being rather fearsome. We stayed at a little hotel in the center of town and did not stray farther than the local markets.

After one night there, we re-boarded the ship and set sail for Cotobato on the island of Mindanao, to visit the mission in Upi. The Tiruray tribe lived up in those parts, and some were known to live in tree houses. After disembarking, we boarded an open-air bus filled with the locals and their wares, including pigs and chickens. We traveled over rough, unpaved roads until we came to the end of the line; there, we transferred to carts drawn by carabaos (water buffalos) to continue the rest of the way.

St. Francis Mission in Upi was a vibrant little compound despite its remote spot. The church itself was made of nipa and bamboo with open sides and roughhewn benches for pews. There was a small organ that had to be hand cranked. Yet the hymns on Sunday morning were sung with as much fervor and enthusiasm as the choirs of a great cathedral. Whenever I hear the hymn "O, Jesus I have Promised," it takes me back to the little nipa church and the hand pumped organ in Upi. We stayed with John and Grace Mears and their infant daughter, Kathleen, in their native-style house. In a few months time the Mearses, and we, would be seeking refuge from the invaders in remote mountain hideaways.

Mother wanted to continue the journey on to Dansalan in Lanao province. This was extremely dangerous territory, but danger didn't deter her. Many hair-raising tales had come out of Lanao. Some said that during the war, the Moros in the mountains were feared more than the Japanese.

We left Upi, got a car and a driver who navigated the almost impassable roads to Dansalan on the shores of Lake Lanao. As we approached the "hotel" where we planned to spend the night, the car was surrounded by swarms of Moros. Their clothing was aflame with color and exquisitely woven designs. Most of the men wore fezzes and carried a kris. The women were dressed in wraparound long skirts with fairly close-fitting blouses. A woven sash draped diagonally across the shoulders to the waist finished the outfit. Some of the men wore long tunics over their loose-legged pants. The little children were half -naked.

It turned out that the crush around the car was more out of curiosity than a move to take us prisoners. The local Datu (chieftain) himself came out to meet us and, after a few pleasantries, we went into the inn. The building was an ornate structure. Intricate carvings adorned the doorways, windows, and railings. Woven tapestries with brilliant colors were hung on the walls. Our room was simply furnished with two cots. A balcony opened up to a view of the beautiful lake. We were served a simple supper of fish, rice, and fruit as we sat on the floor at a low table. We retired early, but during the night were awakened by the pounding of gongs and the sounds of some ceremonial rite.

This trip made an indelible impression on me, and I felt enormously relieved to get back in the car the next morning. Mother, of course, had no such fears. Today, most of these places are out of bounds for Western and even some Filipino travelers since the Moros have increased in numbers and fervor in their drive to become an independent part of the Philippines.

In mid-1941, we took a trip to Manila on the *SS Mayon*. On the deck of the ship docked at the pantalan in Zamboanga, the young army officers at Pettit Barracks were bidding their wives tearful farewells All the families of servicemen had been ordered back to the States for safety. This was not so for the rest of us who were told that the move of service dependents was more or less routine and we weren't to worry. For most of those saying goodbye to their loved ones, it really was farewell. Few, if any, were to see their husbands or wives again.

My father wrote to his mother in England in April 1941:

> The children are feeling the isolation of living in a small place like Zamboanga....I feel fairly sure that we shall be quite ready to leave this place, peaceful and tropical as it is. It is not very good for the children to be so isolated, but they don't notice it so much now as they will in a year or so. Now that the school is closed they are studying with their mother in the mornings. We have a lovely cool porch right facing the sea, so they have a nice place to study. But it is very difficult to enjoy such luxury these days. One's thoughts are constantly on the war and wondering what calamity will stare one on the face in tomorrow's papers.

He goes on to write:

> I do not have a radio and I want one badly, but they are so expensive over here. I am going to get Major Wilson's when he leaves. Of course, most of the broadcasts, apart from the news, is trashy, mostly silly jazz. Fortunately, we do get foreign stations like Shanghai, Singapore and Sidney quite well. Of course, the broadcast from London is perhaps the clearest of all.

Although Daddy mentions loneliness, I have no recollection of feeling that way at all. In my memory, life as a ten-year old was idyllic. In retrospect, though, although there was talk of war, the final days of 1941 were to be the last time I was to feel the carefreeness and freedom I had enjoyed as a child in that land. For the next three years, fear and uncertainty were our constant companions.

The day began as an ordinary Monday. We three children dawdled over breakfast. Afterwards, Geoffrey would be going to Miss Salud Nixon's kindergarten class at the Moro Settlement School. Shirley and I would have our Calvert Home Study laid out for us to do on our own. Mother would be going off to St. John's Chinese School, and Daddy was preparing to go to Brent Hospital for the daily service.

Secretly, Shirley and I were making plans to go across the street to the beach to get in a swim before we tackled the lessons. Angracia, Juliana, and Jeofela, our amahs and house-keeper, could easily be influenced to keep quiet about the plan.

Later, after lunch, I would put on my school uniform of a lavender pleated skirt and white blouse and walk along the sea wall to the Chinese school, which I attended for half of each day. Mother was a firm believer in having us be an integral part of the culture in which she was working.

The routine of the morning's preparations was abruptly broken when a terse announcement came over the radio:

> The Philippines are under a total alert; Pearl Harbor and Luzon have been bombed!

Life in Zamboanga changed on that Monday morning, December 8, 1941. Mother had always said that we'd be glad to eat the foods we disdained when the Japanese came. How did she know? She was to be proved correct. She wrote:

> In all the perils we encountered in the months to follow, none ever held quite the uncertainty and tenseness of the first few weeks. Air raid alarms, false or real, ...we never knew which, broke our sleep and interrupted our waking activity. At first the attacks were elsewhere but our turn might come at any minute.

And it did.

By noon on Monday, there was a mass movement of people. East was going West and South was going North, escaping to the provinces by whatever means they could. We saw ox carts, horse-drawn carts, broken-down buses, little vintas on the sea, and families walking with their earthly possessions carried on their heads pass by our house. Sometimes their household goods would be strung from a bamboo pole and borne by two people. By afternoon the schools were emptied, and we were pondering our options. For the time being, we would hunker down and stay put.

The next few days were spent cutting out squares of black construction paper to fit over the capiz shell panes of our windows. Total blackout would be the rule from now on. Sometimes we rolled bandages for the hospital. Mother and the house girls went to the market to stock up on the fast-dwindling supplies. Usually marketing was done on a daily basis. There was not much refrigeration except the chunk of ice we got once in a while from the icehouse. It wouldn't be long before the market would be emptied of the supplies of food shipped from Manila.

How long would it be before there was nothing to buy and no money with which to buy necessities? We did not have to wait too long for the answers.

Nightly, the air raid siren sounding from Mr. Wilson's ice plant broke the silence. Its wail sent us bolting out of our beds. We took shelter under the wooden front steps, which led up to our porch. To crouch there in pitch blackness, listening to the whine of a plane, not knowing if it were the enemy or a stray fighter plane from Luzon, was a terrifying experience.

We knew that the Americans had only a few planes left after having lost most of them on the ground during a bombing raid at Clark Field on Luzon. Perhaps the first few were stragglers looking for a safe landing in Central Mindanao. Even today, when I hear a siren or the sound of a lone plane in the night, it invokes the feelings of terror that I felt during the first days of the war.

Clearly, a more secure type of shelter needed to be built to replace our temporary spot under the stairs. In the backyard, there was a stand of young acacia trees. Geoffrey, at age six, had already built a tree house amongst their branches to escape from the world! Their leafy tops would provide good camouflage for the shelter underneath. My father, with the help of some hospital personnel, began digging a hole of rectangular dimensions. Completed, it ended up being about ten feet long by five feet wide and about four feet deep. Benches, carved from the earth, ran lengthwise along the sides. A wooden box-like structure supplanted with chicken wire formed the cover. Sand bags combined with branches for camouflage were laid on top. We stocked the shelter with water, some food supplies, and first aid items. The opening faced the house so that we could dive right in when making a run for it.

Taking refuge in the ground made us feel safer. We spent part of many nights there. The grounds of the Philippine Constabulary Barracks abutted our property. Within a few feet from our shelter were the foxholes of those soldiers assigned to the barracks.

From my father's writings:

The Japanese civilian community was not very large and had been interned from the day their country attacked Pearl Harbor. The women and children were put in a schoolhouse near San Ramon and the men were sent over to the island of Basilan and then later to the mainland of Mindanao. The women and children were well treated and received constant supervision of their health by Dr. Tremaine, the army doctor. He and I made a trip out to see them just before Christmas, he to see that their situation was good and I to take toys to the Japanese children. Some Japanese women seemed friendly, others paid no attention. They seemed to know that the day would soon come when their situation would be reversed, and that we would be the prisoners.

Mrs. Price, (a Japanese lady married to an Englishman), the proprietor of the OK Bazaar, who was interned, was most anxious to secure some wool from her store. I was able to get it to her. We instructed the Filipino guard to be kind to them.

The first three weeks were eerie. The town was fairly deserted. Gone from the waterfront were the colorful vintas and the torches of the fishermen at night. News from other islands or abroad was scanty and unreliable. We boxed up valuables in the house. We packed emergency suitcases, little rattan cases, one for each of us. Surely, this conflict would not be long, we thought. A tattered remnant of the packing list I made out shows that we had no idea that what we jammed into those little suitcases would have to last more than three years. Three years later, I would still be wearing the remnants of: *Two shirts, one pair of shoes, seven ribbons, two prs. of shorts, two skirts, six dresses, five underpants, and four prs. socks.* Mother took me aside and refreshed me from time to time about my obligations as the oldest. A few years earlier in Manila when we housed the Nanking refugees, we heard firsthand about the atrocities endured there. Mother was fearful that there might be a repeat performance. We took off rings and jewelry and hid them. Mother had me memorize the combination of the safe as well as the addresses in the States of our church headquarters and relatives. She told me that as the eldest, I would be in charge of my siblings should anything happen to her and my father. I was ten years old and took her instructions seriously.

Overnight my life had changed from one of a carefree childhood in an island paradise to one filled with anxiety and fear. There were no assurances that everything would be fine. There were no answers. Only questions. We had lived in oblivion, thinking that America was omnipotent. In reality, the events of the previous few days had left us powerless, exposed as we were to an uncertain future. In a matter of hours, we had been cut off from the world. Radio reports were sketchy and barely audible.

However, it was almost Christmas. Preparations were cut to a minimum. Yet, for the children, there was still a sort of innocent sense of anticipation.

Christmas in the Philippines had been a wonderful season of fiestas, lanterns, gift giving, and religious celebration. Three Kings' Day marked the end of the festivities. This year, there would be darkness where there had been light. A composition of mine, written a short time after we came to the States, demonstrates that an innovative answer to the darkness we experienced could be found right at our own doorstep:

Firefly Christmas

Christmas 1941 came to Zamboanga. In past Christmases it had been a season of colorful paper lanterns with flowing streamers decorating the fronts of houses or being paraded through the streets. It was a season of fiestas, of song, of candles and pageants celebrated in the traditional way with twelve days ending with Three Kings' Day on January sixth.

Christmas 1941 came to a changed town. Windows were blackened, many of the populace had fled to the mountains. Gone were the crowds in the marketplace. Gone were the shoppers at the OK Bazaar, and gone were the vintas with their brightly colored sails. Fear, uncertainty, and terror paralyzed those who were left. Yet, it was, after all, Christmas.

Tradition in some small way must be carried out, even if it was only to calm the fears of the children. At Brent, the mission hospital, it was customary to sing carols through the wards on Christmas Eve, with the choristers carrying candles. How could this be done when the town was under total blackout?

In front of the hospital was a tree that seemed to be alive with fireflies. I thought that perhaps the light from these insects might be enough to make it possible to see the words of the music.

Christmas Eve morning I went to the hospital laboratory and asked for some test tubes, some gauze and some rubber bands. I proceeded to the firefly tree. Into each tube I put some leaves and eight to ten insects and covered the tops with gauze secured with the elastic. I hadn't been at it long when the air raid siren went off and I had to seek shelter in the building. After the "all clear" had sounded I went out to continue the task I had begun. Again the siren sounded, and again I ran for cover. Fortunately none of the alarms resulted in air strikes. Nevertheless, it made me very jittery since I was down the street from home. Twenty-five or so test tubes were filled, and set aside for the carol service that night.

Christmas Eve as in Christmases past, the medical personnel, teachers, and others from the mission compound caroled through the hospital, visiting the wards and rooms of the sick. The sparkling and twinkling lights from our test tube lanterns, for a few brief moments, made the war seem very far away indeed.

◆

Early in 1942, I had written about fireflies in a composition I wrote while hiding in the mountains:

Nature's Lanterns

Twinkle, flitter, sparkle, What? A live Christmas tree? No, just a small waxy-leafed bush actually swarming with glimmering insects. In the daytime, this shrub helps form a hedge around the school, but when evening shadows creep on, it distinguishes itself from the rest by harboring these fireflies.

All over the shimmery leaves they crawl, blinking their lights. This foliage looks as if star dust has been sprayed over its leaves. As if in competition with the darkening night, the fireflies gleam as midnight approaches.

Occasionally, father lightning bug will lead his brilliant family in procession across the dirt road. This firefly haven is a landmark for small passing boats on the nearby sea. Not even a war can stop this glittering spray from shedding its light.

◆

Christmas morning we sat around our decorated palm tree and opened a few presents that had been sent a month before from our relatives in England and America. Our parents had never ever made much of Santa Claus, a good thing, too. In the bleak years ahead, it would have been hard to explain the absence of gifts to the younger children. There was an annual reading of "The Night Before Christmas," but no list of wants was ever presented to a department store Santa.

There would be three more Christmases before the war was over. We could not know that then, but in the ones to come, we looked back at this one in a special way. Even with the overtones of war, it was the last semblance of the life we had considered normal.

JANUARY 1, 1942

Dr. Julio Trota of Brent Hospital who lived a few doors down on the waterfront, visited about noon. He, Mother, and Daddy discussed evacuation plans, the availability of gasoline, and places to which we might possibly escape. It was felt that the army could supply the gasoline, at least enough for a trip to the interior. They believed that everyone should go inland. We were too exposed, facing the sea as we were.

As Dr. Trota was about to leave, we heard the roar of planes.

"They're coming over now!" Dr. Trota shouted.

Out over the sea, coming in very low over the water, we could see seven planes. They were flying directly toward our house. Dr. Trota ran for home, and we made a dash for our shelter. The air raid siren didn't go off until after the raid had begun. Everyone had been taken by surprise. The two dogs managed to get to the shelter first, followed by us five and the three Filipina women. Glimpsing out of the shelter, we could see the pilots in the planes and the veritable Rising Sun emblazoned under each wing; the first evidence that the enemy was real and that he was here.

In a moment, we were peppered with thousands of machine gun bullets.

We could hear them bouncing off the tops of the sandbags covering our shelter. We could hear them hitting the galvanized tin roof of the house, metal on metal. The planes circled the city several times and at each rotation returned to spray their deadly cargo. Out of frustration, one of the soldiers in the foxhole nearest us began firing at the planes, giving away his position and giving all of us an extra dose of bullets.

5 EVACUATION

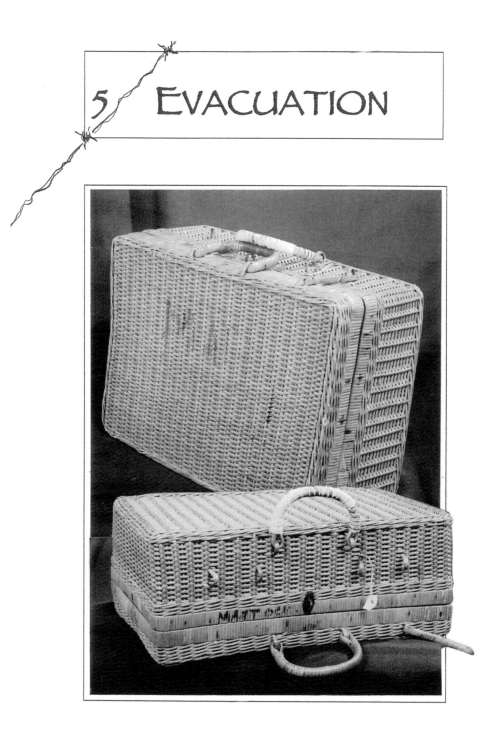

After the "all clear" sounded, we crept out of the shelter. We children picked up the spent bullet cases strewn all over the yard. The sides of the school bus parked in the yard were pockmarked with holes.

My parents were in a quandary about the next step. We felt that the attack might be a prelude to an invasion, and certainly we would be vulnerable living on the sea front as we were. Some officers from the military post came by to offer what assistance they could. We requested a tank of gasoline and a cable to stateside relatives. Later, we learned that the cable the officers sent was the last time my grandmother heard from us for over three years, despite several postcards we filled out, courtesy of the Japanese and the International Red Cross.

A teacher in our school offered her home in Tetuan, a few kilometers out of the city, for the night. She and her family were going further inland. We threw what we could gather quickly into the school bus: the emergency suitcases, rice, canned goods, documents. We set the monkeys free, let the ducks go, and boarded the bus with our family, the Filipina household help, the two dogs Whitey and Brownie (who had been previously been named Whiskey and Brandy by others), and the cat.

We all felt a bit safer going somewhere away from the waterfront. We spent the night crowded on an upper porch in Tetuan. Our hosts had laid out what seemed like a feast. The next morning when it became apparent that the invading army had not arrived, we ventured back to the house on Cawa Cawa. The most traumatic event for us children on that trip was having the cat jump out of the window and scamper off into the fields.

Between air raid sirens, alternating with "all clears," we loaded up the bus with mosquito nets, mattresses, and other necessary items. We had been offered shelter in Cabaluay, a few kilometers out of town. Actually, no one felt safe anywhere, but constant moving kept our minds off the real fear. It seemed that everybody else had the idea of going to Cabaluay. The roads were clogged with every conceivable kind of transportation, and we witnessed novel ways of carting one's possessions.

We stayed at our teacher friend's house in Cabaluay a few nights. Offering all kinds of food and places to sleep, the Filipinos were immensely kind to us. We felt though that we were endangering them, and perhaps it would be better if we could find some place in the remote interior. We did not want our friends to be accused of having harbored us.

Mrs. Enriquez, a teacher in the school, came to our aid. Her father, Mr. Niebert, was a Spanish-American War veteran who had stayed in the Islands and had married a Filipina. He enjoyed prospecting for gold and ore and had built himself a fairly substantial house of nipa and bamboo up in the hills behind the barrio of Malayal, thirty-five miles up the coast. Mrs. Enriquez had never been there herself, but said that we were welcome to it for as long as we needed it.

Since Malayal was beyond paved roads, electricity, and other modern conveniences, we were at somewhat of a loss as to how to get there.

We loaded everyone and our hastily-gathered belongings into the bus and made our way back to Zamboanga City. Daddy felt that the officers at Pettit Barracks might be able to help. He went to Colonel Dalton, the Commander of the small army post, and laid our problem before him. Colonel Dalton had lots of matters before him, not the least of which were the remoteness of his post, the separation from the rest of the forces, and the depressing news from the North; but he was anxious to help. We were all in a desperate situation. Since New Year's Day, we had had no word of the whereabouts of the rest of our mission staff. We all felt a sense of abandonment. The colonel did what he could. He offered a launch to take us up the coast to this place called Malayal.

While my father was in the office of Colonel Dalton, Mr. Gulbranson, the leader of the Christian and Missionary Alliance group, came in with the same request. Mr. Gulbranson already knew about Malayal, as the C&MA group had done missionary work there. He reported that there was a church, a schoolhouse, a pastor, and Subanos who spoke English, all signs favorable to our arrival. The group Mr. Gulbranson represented was already halfway up the coast at a place called Labuan, a small town at the end of the road that led north along the shore. The men agreed to join forces. We would pick up the thirty-two of them at Labuan on our way.

This time, we gathered together some first aid supplies, garden tools, axes, pots and pans, canned goods, staples—even school books—and loaded them onto the launch. As we were about to set off at dusk, there appeared on the dock, two people who begged us to include them. They were an Austrian Jewish refugee couple who had been traveling in the Far East selling watches and jewelry. They were caught in Zamboanga in their travels; and because of the big red "J" on their passports, they were as nervous about the coming of the Japanese as we were. We welcomed them aboard. Their trunk-loads of trinkets were a source of fascination for us children.

We were now ready: our family, the three Filipinas, Mooshie and Gustav Handel, and the two dogs.

The cadre of several officers posted to Pettit Barracks came to the dock to bid us bon voyage. Cut off from supplies and reinforcements, it would fall to them and the brave band of Filipino Scouts to defend the city from the might of the Japanese army. Now, knowing what befell most of them, it makes me even sadder to remember them waving until they became specks on the fading landscape.

Our night at sea, as the *Aurora* traveled without lights, proved to be a wild one. We were tossed about by mountainous waves as our vessel hugged the shoreline. At one point, a can of red paint broke loose and washed the deck from stem to stern. Sunrise brought relief when we got our bearings, although the sea was far from calm. The captain had to be convinced to stop at Labuan for the others. He didn't want to be caught by a Japanese patrol boat with this particular cargo. From my father's writings:

> Hugging the shore, we chugged along in the swiftly fading twilight. We were starting out on a trek that would last a long time. It seemed like entering a great solitude as we went into the night—even nature itself reflected from the darkening hills beyond

represented the obscurity of our future, yet underneath we felt, were the everlasting arms of God.

The captain of the launch had little knowledge of the coastline. After four hours he shut off his engine scanning the dark shore looking for Labuan. Without the light of the moon it was impossible to make out anything in the coconut groves that lined the beach.

The launch pitched and rolled mercilessly. The Handels were frightfully sick and were sure we were going to sink. Our children who have always been good sailors, staggered along the pitching decks trying to comfort poor Mr. and Mrs. Handel. The Filipina girls were knocked out by the violent motion of the boat and were flat on their backs in the wheelhouse. We spent a miserable night waiting for the dawn that would reveal our position of proximity to Labuan and the waiting American missionaries.

Getting the others who were waiting on the beach at Labuan onto the anchored launch proved to be tricky. The *Aurora* rolled from side to side in the pounding surf. Among the group on the shore waiting to be picked up was an elderly couple, a disabled man, thirteen children, and some of the household help from the mission at Tetuan: altogether about thirty-five or so. Several bancas (small outriggered boats) filled with passengers braved the waves on the short distance to the anchored launch. Finally, Filipino boys swam out to hold the little boats steady while everyone climbed aboard a rope ladder hung over the side. The cargo was hoisted aboard by these same swimmers. Although everyone and everything was soaked, the boarding was successful.

We pitched and heaved (literally) up the coast for four more hours feeling emboldened by our numbers. Certainly for us children, life looked a little brighter with the thought of having playmates. For our parents, the burdens of providing a life in this remote and mountainous place would be shared.

From Mother's writings:

The green hills, fronted with jagged gray crags, fringed

with white surf, made a scene of rugged beauty. The Eternal God is our refuge, and underneath are the everlasting arms.

We breathed freely already. The process of unloading the launch into the little bancas that came out to take us and our goods to shore was made difficult because of the pounding surf. At times, the bancas were tossed about on the rolling waves like pieces of driftwood. Some of the loaded boats became swamped. As a result, we spent the next few hours drying out everything. This drying-out scene was to be repeated time and again for the duration of the war.

We waved good-bye to the departing launch, our last connection with Zamboanga, and faced the mountains.

6 MALAYAL

Cogon Cottage

The gentle Subano tribe inhabited this part of the coast and inland through the jungle and up the steep mountain trails. The Christian and Missionary Alliance group had been to these parts before. There was a pastor and a small church among the nipa houses that lined the shore. Further down the shore was a Chinese tienda in a fairly substantial wooden and coconut frond building. My parents were able to communicate with Kau-ah, the owner of the store, as he spoke Amoy. The tienda had a broad, well-worn wooden counter. Such items as rice; desiccated coconut; sugar; palay (unhusked rice); and "am pao be," a kind of candy made with brown sugar and puffed rice, were among the items for sale. Yard goods were also available. Kau-ah knew about Mr. Niebert's shack up in the mountains and told us it was a fine one and would be suitable for our family.

In the meantime, we were all quartered in a schoolhouse on the beach. Surrounding the school was a beautiful garden filled with both vegetables and brilliant flowers. Even today, when I smell freshly grown tomatoes, I am taken back to the fragrance of that garden. A beautiful bed of red flowers similar to that of a rooster's coxcomb was ablaze at the back of the property. Inside the nipa school, we staked out spaces for our family and laid out our bedrolls. The Subanos brought us food and cooked for us outside in the schoolyard.

Meanwhile, my parents tried to find a guide who knew about the shack and who could lead them up the trail to it. The other missionary group set about trying to find a suitable spot away from the shore to build their encampment. They eventually settled on a place up the Salupit River about two miles from the beach.

From my father's writings:

> Samsun, a native Subano, was chosen to lead us and Mr. Handel up to the shack. It was a fine day and we got

started well before noon. For a mile or so we walked along the dusty trail parallel with the beach...a thin wall of vegetation and trees partially shielded us from the view of the ocean. It was an ideal spot, so peaceful and hidden and yet capable by man of being turned into a bloody slaughterhouse. If only one could live forever in peace with the blue indigo sea to gaze upon and the restful eternity of the hills shielding us. Illusion-daydreams come to lick our sores, but we cannot rest. Life is a struggle, a battle.

We plugged on in the hot sun, Samsun leading. Higher and higher we climbed, sometimes entering deep forest gloom, sometimes emerging into a clearing with bright sunshine and endless views of the distant sea. From some vantage point we would in one sweep of the eye, catch some of the beauty and majesty of Mindanao, virgin forests everywhere and gold, some people thought!

The climbers refreshed themselves with water from the coconuts that the guide opened with a sharp bolo (machete). About an hour into the climb, a huge snake slithered across the path. That was enough for Mr. Handel to say that the idea of finding the shack should be abandoned. At that point, he turned around and said that his wife and the children would never be able to make it. Yet, my parents plugged onward, figuring if Mr. Niebert could do it, so could they.

From my father's writings:

Eventually we sighted the house standing in a field of cogon grass like a great plateau, with the deep forest behind it. Encroaching to within an arch of twenty-five feet from the house on one side and extending out on the other side was a dense tropical forest. We welcomed this curtained protection around three sides of us, although its impenetrableness and hidden steep ravines seemed repellent. To the west and north the house faced Sibuco Bay. We would enjoy and unobstructed view of seventy miles out to sea.

At first glance, my parents knew it would be perfect. It was constructed of nipa and bamboo and set up on stilts about ten feet off the ground. Underneath in a trellised area, Mr. Niebert's rock collection was displayed. These specimens were all carefully labeled and numbered. At the rear of this underground area was a crudely-constructed compartment that housed the privy.

One entered the upstairs by a bamboo ladder stairway. The main room was a combination eating and living area, and the only furniture was a table and some bamboo and rattan chairs. The floor was bamboo slats. Keeping the floor clean was, of course, going to be a simple matter.

At the back of the living area was a bedroom which ran the width of the house. The floor was a springy woven bamboo matting. Actually, once our bedding was in place, it was quite comfortable to sleep on the floor. To the right of the eating area were two small bedrooms with wide shelves attached to the walls that served as beds. On the left as one entered, was the kitchen. It was equipped with a sandbox-like platform upon which some rocks were strategically placed to hold pots. A couple of shelves completed the room. Off the kitchen was a porch where some large galvanized iron tubs were placed for catching rainwater.

The windows were bamboo and nipa flaps which were held open with bamboo poles. The front door, likewise, was nipa; a toggle bolt kept it closed. In time, Daddy constructed some shelving and made a couple of small bamboo stools.

Life was going to be different for us. There was no electricity. There was no running water or refrigeration. We were going to have to learn fast to live as the native Subanos did. We had brought some staples with us, but there was no way to replenish any of these once they ran out.

Samsun showed my parents where we could get fresh water from a clear mountain spring about three hundred yards from the house. The spring itself, which bubbled out of a rock, was down a somewhat slippery slope. But the water was crystal clear and cool. Bathing and clothes washing would have to take place at the Lanote Creek, a mile down a trail through thick forestation.

My parents were considerably buoyed by the condition in which they found the area and soon returned to the shore to report to the others that our quarters had been secured. Meanwhile, the Handels were trying to buy a house from the natives on the shore for a few pesos and some trinkets. But none was to be had.

Daddy went back up to the shack a day or two after the original inspection to make sure all was in order. He describes the night he spent there alone:

> The night alone there in the mountain wilderness was no joy, for as the twilight turned to dark, I became tangibly aware that the nearby forest was alive with tropical mysteries. Birds of great size, big blue-black birds squawking an awful din, swooped by the shack just about sunset. The air was full of bats with their uncanny resemblance to flying rats. The ground around the shack seemed to be crawling with poisonous reptiles. The great concert of cicadas began to rise about sundown. From the black forest came the dying shrieks from animals caught in some sudden death struggle. Together with the tremendous crescendo of the cicadas, one could scarcely think. Below it all was the thunderous chorus of nocturnal insects turning the forest into a roaring ocean of noise. Far away, at intervals, came the occasional booming of the surf down below.
>
> The whole atmosphere was completely alien, surrounded as I was with the tall grass and the fantastic trees. One could not shut it out entirely, for the cracks in the floor were an open invitation to snakes. There seemed to be too much to cope with. One could see how spiritism and demonism seemed more natural when one is opposed by such real or imagined forces.

He continues:

> I was glad to see the family coming up the trail the next day. I met them at the "banana house," so named because over time when we stopped the natives would give us bananas which we ate under the shade of their

trees. The children were not riding carabaos as I had expected, nor were they very tired. I had underestimated their hiking ability. The carabao was huffing and puffing because he had been away from water for a time. After a short rest, we all climbed the rest of the way to the shack. It was good to feel that we had arrived at last to the new house. But all our thoughts were tempered with the awful uncertainty of the future.

In honor of the razor-sharp grass that one had to navigate everywhere, we named the house "Cogon Cottage." In the end, the Handels did join us, as did our three Filipina amahs and housekeepers. We were a group of ten.

A composition I wrote in 1943 in the Davao Internment Camp somewhat describes the ubiquitous cogon grass:

Our Life in Malayal

When we first went to the hills, the cogon grass was growing right up to the front door of our house. Because of this we named the place, "Cogon Cottage." Cogon grass is a very interesting plant. If you walk through it you may get cut, and you will get very itchy. It grows very fast and has tough roots.

My Mother's house girls, Angracia, Jeofila, and Julita (whom we took with us because they had no place to go after the machine gunning) used to work very hard with bolos to cut the grass down. After they left, Daddy and a Subano boy worked on it and little by little they cut it away.

One day we decided to burn it because the wind was right. We all helped to beat back the flames with green branches of trees and shrubs. Soon the whole field was cleared and we had a lovely place to play.

◆

We had fled to the mountains without toys; we had no dolls or other playthings. How thrilled we were to have, "a lovely place to play!" We didn't miss the conventional trappings of childhood, but managed to create games and playthings out of what was at hand. With a bit of fabric from Kau-ah's tienda, I made a rag doll and sketched a rather realistic-looking face on her. With other scraps I made her a quilt. The Subano children shared their yo-yos. Baseball was played with a stick and a beanbag.

We children were excited by the new house and made a quick inspection of everything. A small cement bodega was situated about a hundred yards from the main house. We'd have fun playing in it during rainy season, we thought.

However, we soon found out that mountain life was going to be a family effort. The first problem was water. We were all assigned a bamboo pole, each according to his height. We went to the spring twice a day and filled our tubes using a coconut shell to scoop up the water from the little pool. Sometimes the trip back home would be harrowing over the muddy trail, and it was all we could do to keep the tube upright. Once home, we would empty the water into a big tub on the back porch. In addition, when it rained, we raced to put out pails and pots to catch the water. Hearing rain in the middle of the night, Mother would cry out, "Man the pans!"

When a new day dawned, it brought with it a busy routine of domesticities. Fires had to be started on the stove. Of course, in order to make the fires, many hours of collecting kindling and wood chopping had to have occurred.

From Daddy's writings:

There was deadwood lying about everywhere in the forest which had to be freed from live trees and toilsomely dragged through a maze of prickly vines. Once a tree was dragged out into the open trail, the worst was over except for dragging it up to the shack. It was chopped to pieces with a very inadequate hatchet.

We children awoke every morning to the sound of Daddy grating coconuts. From somewhere, he had obtained a three-legged stool with a metal grater-like prong, attached. The husk was removed from the coconut and reserved for fuel. The coconut water was poured out through a hole in the shell and saved for drinking. Then the coconut was split open and, half at a time, was scraped over the metal prong to produce white flaky meat. The first gratings were used for the top of cereal. The second layer was put into a mesh bag with a little warm water and squeezed. The resulting liquid was used for "cream" for coffee. More liquid was added to the residue and this was used for cereal and other dishes. The remainder was then boiled and the oil it produced was used for cooking or for the oil lamps. Our kerosene had given out early in the year so the discovery of being able to use coconut oil for the lamps was a lifesaver.

The coconut trees did not grow at the altitude at which we were living so it was necessary to make trips to the shore to procure them.

From my father's writings:

Of course, living there day by day was a tremendous experiment. Everyday was more or less a lifetime. We had to learn to adjust ourselves to an environment that was completely alien to us. We were very fortunate in discovering certain kinds of food, particularly the coconut. Really, the coconut is one of God's greatest gifts. We hadn't been there very long before the natives told us we could have all the coconuts we could carry. The owner of a plantation on the shore would send a boy up a tree and cut the coconuts for us. We would tie them together. I would carry four in each hand and two around my neck. Mrs. Mattocks would carry the same. The children would carry two or three. We would then go back staggering up the mountain, a two hour trip!

I remember those coconut details well; we children did not look forward to that trudge in the hot sun. Of course, we did look forward to a stop at the "Banana House" on the way back.

In addition to the preparation of the coconut, there was the grinding of corn, rice, and coffee beans. We had obtained a heavy stone grinder from some of the natives on the beach who lugged it up the mountains for us. It was an invaluable addition to our meager kitchen supply. The Subanos showed us the cassava root. When dried, it was ground into fine flour. Tapioca was also a byproduct of this root. Corn was ground into flour and used to make pancakes.

One of the daily chores was the removal of the brown husks from the palay (unhusked rice). To accomplish this, the palay was put into a hollowed-out place on a sturdy log about five feet long and at least a foot in diameter. Then, a pestle-like pole was used to separate the rice grains from the husks. We took turns using the pole to pound the palay placed in the scooped out place on the log. Then, the grains and the husks were put into a winnowing basket and were tossed into the air, letting the husks blow away. No one had to explain to us what "separating the wheat from the chaff" meant. As in the case of the bamboo water carriers, each one of us had a "pestle" according to his height with which to do our share of the pounding.

Every once in a while, Mother would get very brave and make the trip down to the Chinese tienda on the beach. She would return with yard goods, sugar, and some treat like bucayo, a candy made from brown sugar and coconut. On one of these trips, she ran into Hassim, one of the Moro school boys from St. Alban's. He greeted her warmly and asked her to wait while he swam out to his vinta. He soon returned with some mangoes.

Sometimes Kau-ah, the Chinese merchant at the tienda on the beach, would send up some beef. Two Subanos would carry it swinging on a pole between them. Of course, we had no refrigeration, so after one or two meals of roast beef, Mother would set to work cutting the meat into strips and drying it in the sun. We would use this "tapa" sparingly until the next donation of meat. On occasion, the Subanos would bring us a slab of pork. We cut the meat into strips and strung it up over the smoky stove where it would hang for days. Once in a while, we were served a treat of this "bacon."

Much of our time was spent scouring the countryside for anything we could buy or barter for in the way of something to eat: eggs, vegetables, or fruit.

According to my father:

It was always an encouraging sound to hear someone coming up the trail with food. Along with the barter for price went a little friendly visit that soon broke down all the barriers of strangeness and made us feel one with the remote mountain tribe.

We set to work making gardens. The Subanos were very helpful in this respect, giving us advice as well as seeds and seedlings. Clearing the land of the fast-growing cogon grass continued to be a problem. The grass cut deeply into the skin leaving us with great red gashes. Our only defense against these cuts was a thorough cleansing with strong laundry soap, which we saved for medicinal purposes. The cuts and gashes soon festered. In time, we all had painful tropical ulcers eating into the flesh on our legs and feet. But the cultivation of vegetables was necessary for survival. We grew mongo beans, tomatoes, peppers and camotes (sweet potatoes), and onions. We children grew a few vegetables on our own little plots. Because of raids by wild animals, the garden had to be fenced in with bamboo poles lashed with rattan.

The Subanos were a generous and friendly group; we realized how dependent we were on them for sustenance as well as protection from the enemy. However, one of their practices really grated on Mother's nerves. They used slash and burn techniques to clear the mountainsides so they could plant their crops, especially corn and camotes. We just ached listening to the sound of the felling of the great forest trees. Huge mountainsides were laid barren in a short time. No amount of explaining and cajoling could convince them to alter their methods, which had been ingrained for centuries. After the trees were cut, the burning would take place. These barren mountainsides or "kaingens," as they were called, left the landscape scarred and charred. In our year in the hills, most of the area surrounding us was denuded in this way.

From Daddy's recollections:

A source of trouble began to develop when the natives began to chop down trees. We were surrounded by these tremendous, large hardwood trees that provided a wonderful shade especially down around the well making the water nice and cool. The trees being felled would sometimes come down in the night and take with them a lot more trees. The night air was punctuated by these explosions and cracklings of falling trees. These people lived by making kaingens. They simply wanted a quick turn around of their crops of camotes. Leaving these barren spots in the mountains was rather depressing. We wondered how long it would be perhaps, before we were cut off the precious supply of water....

At times, there was tension when the Handels were able to obtain foodstuffs from the Subanos by trading the jewelry and trinkets in their trunks. The glittering baubles were more attractive than the few aspirin tablets we had to offer. For a time, there were problems concerning the meting out of food. It was suggested that perhaps the children, being smaller, should not receive a whole banana! These problems were worked out to everyone's satisfaction eventually.

Life soon settled into a predictable rhythm. Always at the forefront was the caring for the garden, the gathering of produce, bartering with the Subanos for fruits and other products, and the preparation of meals.

We had only primitive utensils, many of which were made from coconut shells. There was no way to store food. I do remember Mother working hard over the smoky fire trying to make the meals palatable and giving familiar names to all the concoctions she made for the family. For all the years Mother had been in the Philippines before this, someone else had shopped for food and made the meals, as she was working full time at the school. Therefore, the mountain experience was all the more daunting because the daily production of meals was unfamiliar to her. It is amazing to realize how quickly my parents adapted to this primitive life.

From my diary:

....We dry meat and cassava. We open a rusty can of Carnation milk. It was still good. We opened a package of Rice Krispies, a year and a half old. All the puffed had escaped and only half a package was left.

Here's an entry which shows that sometimes we behaved as ordinary children, despite all the hard work we had to perform.

....Handel's bed fell. Us [sic] children were laughing very much because we could hear it cracking and kept jumping whenever it did. Mother kept telling us to lie down but we just couldn't. Finally, with a KLOP it fell. Laughter was great. Daddy fixed the bed. Later we read *Midsummer's Night's Dream*.

Gardening became a discouraging proposition. The carabaos soon discovered this source of food and in the dead of night would lumber across the fields and plunder the produce. They would trample everything in sight. At first, the dogs would chase them away, but they soon grew bored. We'd line up rocks at all the windows and as soon as we heard the thundering hooves, we would hurl the rocks out into the darkness. I don't know how many hit their mark as it was pitch black, but we did have a couple of night's peace after a rock attack. One night, they chewed up some precious petates (straw mats) that we had left out to dry.

It was always exciting when the natives brought food. They brought us some chickens, which were soon named. Remedia was given her name because she was exchanged for some medicine. We cleared the shelves of Mr. Niebert's rock collection under the house and made chicken coops and roosts. The roosters were named Spangled and Banner. In addition to all the forest noises, we had to accustom ourselves to the clucking and crowing right underneath our beds. We children, of course, were miserable when it came time to put one of our named "pets" into the pot. The following is a composition I wrote in 1942 about one of our favorite hens:

Pix and Her Chix

During the war we evacuated to a place called Balatacan (a district of Malayal). It is about 30 miles from Zamboanga. Balatacan is in the mountains. For marketing we go over to the barren kaingens (barren clearings where the Subanos plant corn and camotes) to collect fruits, vegetables and eggs. One day while going to get food we bought Mother a hen. We called this hen, Pixie.

Pixie would not lay eggs so we said we would put her in the pot. I caught Pixie and tied her up but she escaped. I saw her disappear into the tall cogon grass. My father, brother and I followed her into where we saw her disappear. We found an ideal nest there with a back door and a front door. There were nine eggs under her. I took her home and my sister took the eggs and let her stay in a box. Three weeks later we heard little peeps. Underneath the mother hen was a wet, scrawny chick. During the night we heard many peeps and in the morning when I went to open the chicken boxes (we had to close them because of the wild cats) I saw nine scrawny chicks. Later at ten o'clock they had become nine beautiful chicks. We called them, Primrose, Polly, Peter, Patricia, Pinocchio, Phoebe, Peachy, Penny and Piña (which means pineapple in Spanish).

◆

Another description of "Our Chicken Farm" written in Davao Internment Camp follows:

Our Chicken Farm

We had about twenty-five chickens up in the hills, and we had names for every one. Mine were: Blondie, Marigold and Susanna. Geoffrey's hen was Blueberry, who took the prize for egg laying with one hundred and seven eggs. Shirley's hens were Minnie who laid thirty eggs and Remedia because we traded some medicine for her.

◆

Some entries from my diary:

....Primrose missing. Dodong came with tomatoes and apo. He stayed so long. Always snooping and looking around. "How much this? How much that? How much you pay your ring?" Indian tells us that Dodong is accused of snitching. We find Polly dead with eggs inside her. Samsun brought up two bunches of bananas. Swarms of locusts blacken the sky. They make loud humming sound. They chew up our garden!

....Nice sunny morn. Lumegut came with bananas. Bongalo boys came with bananas, papayas and eggs. Indian brought go-go. For supper we had leftover roast. The GO sign is up on bananas.

....One year ago since we saw Zamboanga. It is very windy this morning. Blows nipa all over the place. We cleaned the big bedroom. My, it was dirty! The shelves look much better. Geoffrey and I went to the "woodlands" to get wood. I went to Samsun's to see if I could get a little petate made for Shirley. It was too expensive. So I shall have to ask Nacida. We went to the river for baths.

....Drizzly rain. Misty. I stayed in bed. Mother tells me I have "Amebia". [I must have meant "anemia."]

....Carabaos came last night. I cleaned Shirley's shelf because she wanted it like mine. Anita came for treatment. We read *Midsummer's Night's Dream*, from Shakespeare. We make bibingka.

Wash day and bathing presented a problem. As I mentioned previously, Lanote Creek was a strenuous walk down a steep mountain path through thick forestation. A trip to do laundry and bathing was an afternoon's work.

Carrying the load of wet washing up the slippery mountain path was tricky. All the family participated in the laundry ritual. Drying clothes was difficult. We laid them out on the rocks after they were washed so that they would dry. But not much sun reached the river bank. In the rainy season, we hung them all over the house. Actually, we only had a few clothes. We girls wore shorts and tops. Dresses were reserved for Sunday. Our shoes began to wear out and we wore native bakyas. A composition of mine from that time best describes the Lanote trips.

Wash Day in the Wilds

With tubs of dirty clothes on our heads, we walked for miles to do the wash. To get to the Lanote River we walked through fields of tall cogon grass, sometimes ten feet high. If a blade scratched one, an infected sore which we called a "tropical ulcer" would soon appear. From the fields of grass, we would walk deeper into woods and dark forest down stony and slippery trails. Squads of chattering monkeys would jump from tree to tree chattering wildly as afraid of us as we were of them. Sometimes we'd hear the plaintive cry of a deer and a huge stag would cross our path in fear. There were tracks in the trail which told us that wild boar had been foraging there on a previous night. We saw only one of these ugly creatures. We were glad he didn't use the horn on the end of his nose on us! Colorful birds flitted in the air above us and gorgeous parakeets, parrots and cockatoos showed off their brilliant colors before us.

There were mighty forest trees with trunks eight feet in diameter. From the trunks wide buttresses fanned out and planted themselves in the ground. Priceless orchids swayed in the breeze from these towering monsters and many beautiful plants clung to the bark of these trees, parasites that they were.

Soon, the swift flowing mountain stream came into view. Clear, cool water dashed over rocks and stones on its way to the sea. After the hot trudge through the forest with our loads it was a welcome and refreshing sight.

Immediately we set to work building a circular wall of rocks in the river with tiny openings for the water to flow through. Into this improvised tub we'd put the clothes. The swirling stream passing through served as our washing machine. While the clothes were swirling around we children would jump into the water, for this was our only opportunity to bathe. When the clothes were soaked we would take them out and spread them on rocks and pound them with a stone just as we had seen the natives do. For soap we used the bark of a vine called, "go go." It made mountainous suds and for that it made us feel better about cleanliness.

After a while, we laid the clothes on rocks or hung them in branches to dry a bit. While waiting for this, we children had fun trying to catch shrimps in coconut shell traps we had made. In a few hours it was time to start our trek up the mountain. On the trip up we did not frolic and skip as we had on the way down for we all carried heavy damp clothing in baskets on our heads. Woe to him or her who dropped a clean piece of laundry onto the trail. While laundry day was always arduous, the thought of the refreshing swim and shrimp trapping at the end of the trail was something we looked forward to.

◆

Another composition written about that time describes an experience on the mountain trail:

An Encounter with a Snake

As my thoughts come to me, I recollect going to the river with my mother's washing. On a lonely mountain path through the forest were many dark trees and graceful vines. Here and there wild begonias grew. Monkeys jumped in the branches above us and our dog bounded ahead chasing butterflies. As I was walking down the trail, I saw a snake next to a dark giant tree. My legs trembled. My heart went "thump, thump." I ran down the trail to where my mother was (I always loved to linger behind). I told her my story exaggerating greatly, telling her I had seen a snake as big as a forest tree.

When we came back up I showed my mother the snake. It turned out to be a big vine, six inches in diameter. I laughed at myself. Imagine being afraid of a vine! I found out that the name of the vine was, "go go." We scraped the insides and the shreds were like soap. When put in water it bubbles and acts like soap. From then on we used go go bark to wash the clothes. It made us think we were using soap.

◆

Every day Mother set aside time for schoolwork. We would go to the bodega mentioned earlier so that we felt that we were actually going to a school. We did arithmetic problems, usually related to the life we were leading. We wrote compositions, diary entries, and read to each other. The books we read were mostly the classics: Shakespeare plays, books of poetry and history. We read the Bible and memorized verses. One exercise entailed writing to our grandmothers in America and England; the letters we never sent gave us practice in the art of letter writing. At one point I had a "school" for Geoffrey and Shirley. I planned lessons for them and corrected the papers. They went along with this activity, amazingly enough. We made friends amongst the Subano children; and they, in turn, taught us their games, told us about their customs. Most of them spoke English, taught to them in their little mountain school.

We were ever fearful of becoming ill or contracting some dreaded tropical disease. We had little medicine, and among our combined group, no medical personnel. The biggest problem we had was that of tropical ulcers. The slightest cut or scratch turned into an infected sore that penetrated deeply into the flesh. One of the Subanos told us of a native cure. It was to take the white membrane that covers the inside of an egg shell and place it over the sore. It acted as sort of a poultice and did work in some cases to relieve the throbbing. Another of the local "cures" was to take the leaves of the guava tree, soak them, and then apply them to the infected area.

Occasionally, we children had fevers and colds. I was plagued with fevers and sore throats a great deal of the time. However, we were spared malaria, dengue, and other tropical ailments. Once, on one of our trips down the mountain, Geoffrey fell on a shattered log and sustained a huge gash in his leg. Mother took out hundreds of splinters. To clean the wound, she used some of the strong laundry soap that we had saved, and bound the gash up as well as she could. For several days, we waited anxiously and hoped that no infection would occur. Thankfully, none did. In later years when we came back to the States, Geoffrey made a little money on the side by charging his fifth grade classmates a nickel to see the scar resulting from an enemy saber slash! Toothpaste soon ran out so we used crushed charcoal as tooth powder. My father sharpened his razor blades by rubbing them in a circular motion on the inside of a glass tumbler.

Night falls early in the tropics. We looked forward to our evenings around the dining table with its flickering coconut shell oil lamp giving off the only light. Charades, ghost, guessing games, Chinese checkers, and rummy filled the hour before bed. We sang songs and Mother always read something from the classics. The Handels were anxious to improve their English. In turn, my parents wanted to bone up on their German. We had many laughs as we tried to carry on in each other's language.

From my father's writings:

It was cozy in the shack at night. When the coconut oil lamp was lit after sunset and the supper dishes were washed up, we used to gather around the table in what we called the dining room and play rummy. The Handels were always good sports about playing games and although Mrs. Handel had a hard time remembering when she should play her card, this only increased the fun. Very often the card game would be interrupted by someone hearing an unusual sound outside. After intense practice at listening, we got so we could easily identify the variety of night noises.

Sometimes in the short tropical twilight, we would sit outside on a wooden bench. The Handels would entertain us with stories of their life in Vienna before the war. The stories usually had to do with food and many succulent descriptions were given us of all the excellent dishes served in Vienna. All the wonderful menus only served to make us yearn for the day when we should get choice, palatable meals again.

It was comforting to know that two kilometers down the trail was "Forest Glen," the camp of the Christian and Missionary Alliance group. Each family, with the help of the Subanos, built its own nipa shack. A communal dining shed was built, which also served as a place for services. The compound abutted a fast flowing stream. Unlike our situation, there was always an abundance of water. Circling the back of the encampment was a high ridge. The entire camp was under a canopy of towering trees with huge buttresses securing them to the earth. The group spent much time in the tilling of the soil. Like us, survival for the most part, depended upon raising their own produce. While we were plagued with nightly visits from the carabaos, monkeys plundered their gardens.

Not everyone in the group was originally from Zamboanga. A few were refugees, from French Indochina, who had sought safety in the Philippines. Unlike our family's situation, the divisions of labor in the camp were spread among many. Several women shared the teaching of school held daily. The missionary work that had been done earlier with the Subanos proved to be a great source of comfort and strength to the group, and we reaped its benefits as well.

We children enjoyed our frequent visits to the Glen. We relished playing with the children, especially those of our ages. Forest Glen became the social center of our lives. How we looked forward to these respites in our lives! As children, we did not have the ever-present concerns of our parents, who worried about the future; what the mountains would hold for us; whether the Moros, or the penal colony inmates roaming the hills, or the Japanese to the south would end our lives in that place. There were times, however, when specific rumors, or information the Subanos passed on to us, made me fearful. Our parents never hid anything from us in terms of what lay ahead, but they always discussed events with a positive approach so as not to alarm us unnecessarily. And, as always, they had faith in God that He would watch over us.

And so we celebrated birthdays and holidays and tried to keep some semblance of the normal yearly events that make up life. Cakes were made of cassava or rice flour and decorated with grated coconut. We drew names for presents. I still have a gift of a little wooden hanger with a cover made from scraps of plaid material embroidered with my initials. We copied poetry and made little booklets. Almost every Sunday, we left Cogon Cottage and went down the trails for church services at Forest Glen. Daddy took his turn at preaching. He read prayers from the Book of Common Prayer, and we learned more about the evangelical form of service. Although many of the hymns were the same, we were introduced to the less formal Gospel music. We participated in Sunday School and were diligent about the preparation of lessons. We all memorized Psalm 91 and felt comforted by verse 11: "For He shall give His angels charge over thee, to keep thee in all thy ways."

Every morning my father or mother would conduct a little prayer service. They would read a passage from the Bible and offer a prayer or two. We children were invited to add to the devotions. Mother always added a hymn. We all seemed to be consoled by this daily ritual.

We were always happy when we were permitted to spend a few nights with our friends at the Glen. Pleasures were simple. Arlene and I had our two secret tomato plants up on the ridge between the buttresses of two trees. We nurtured those plants lovingly. Our goal was to keep the boys from finding them. We even invented a code to refer to them to keep their spot secret. At that time, I wrote about a day at the Glen:

Our Picnic at the Glen (1942)

One Saturday morning we were invited to the missionaries' camp for a picnic. Only we girls went on it. We went upstream on a beautiful river to a falls. The father of one of the girls said it was too dangerous so we went a little further upstream. We stopped by a nook beside the river where we decided to rest. The two Filipina girls hid Easter eggs, while we six children took out our dolls and their belongings. The girls' names were: Arlene, Patsy, Peggy, Betty, Cecily and Shirley. We found a tree which was good for hanging dolls' clothes. Soon the Filipina girls called us to find the eggs and eat.

Arlene found the most eggs, and her prize was an extra piece of candy. We had sandwiches and the usual picnic food.

After dinner we made doll clothes. At two o'clock we went bathing and had great fun splashing about in the water. We swam for about an hour and then it was time to go home. We packed up our dolls and clothes and then we were on our way. When we arrived back at camp we were happy and tired.

◆

Although sandwiches are mentioned in the foregoing composition, we did not have traditional bread. We made a sort of flat bread with rice, corn or cassava flour, and water. The resulting batter was "baked" in an iron skillet over hot coals. The "bread" was filled with vegetables or possibly meat. There was no butter or any sort of condiment other than salt to add to the filling.

From my father's writings:

It was always a pleasure to have the visits from the missionaries down below in the valley. They liked to come up as they could get a good day of sunshine. Their camp, built in the forest, was rather gloomy. Sometimes they would stay overnight. There would be a welcome exchange of what news we had, a recounting of anything that had happened in the camps and discussion of any future plans.

In August of 1942, a baby was born at Forest Glen to Mr. and Mrs. Hess. One of the nurses from Zamboanga risked her life to come up to the camp to help in the delivery. She brought some food and medical supplies with her. The baby was named Victor (for victory) Glenn (for the mountain home). It was an exciting time for all of us children. I am sure we didn't fathom the dangers that surrounded the event and the risks Miss Evangelista took to come up the coast, practically under the eyes of the Japanese.

Also, in August of 1942, a German escapee from Luzon, Albert Klestadt, appeared at Forest Glen. He had heard that one of the people in the missionary group was well-versed in navigation, having captained a mission boat. Mr. Klestadt was looking for someone who knew the waters to go with him as he made his way to Australia. Mr. Holesch, one of our group, was a Czechoslovakian who had considerable sea faring experience. The children all loved him. He had a black patch over one eye and told fantastic stories. In the end Mr. Holesch declined to leave the camp to accompany Mr. Klestadt although he did share his considerable knowledge of the waters. At one point Mr. Klestadt came up to visit us at Cogon Cottage for a few days. We kids thought he was a spy and were a bit afraid. I have since found a book written by Mr. Klestadt entitled, *The Sea Was Kind* in which he describes his escape from Luzon. In one chapter, he describes the Forest Glen camp:

> The feats of organization and courage which had produced this camp were amazing, but not unique. In other parts of the islands and elsewhere in the Pacific, similar stories of organized hideouts could be told. What set "Forest Glen " apart was its spirit. The missionaries external circumstances were desperate and they must have known it in their hearts. In Manila and Iloilo I had seen people behave quite differently in the face of the approaching enemy; the men of my type, the businessmen, bankers, engineers, planters and public servants. In many cases they had been afraid, irresolute or had put on a false front of unconcern. Compared to them, these missionaries, these poor relations of the white communities in the Far East, were heroes---that was the only word to describe them---but I don't think they ever thought of themselves as such. (1)

After a sojourn of seven weeks, Mr. Klestadt left and finally made it to Australia. His visit was the only time we ever saw anyone from the foreign community in our thirteen months of hiding.

From our vantage point high in the mountains, we could observe Japanese warships plying the coast. Often warplanes flew overhead. Every time there were planes Mrs. Handel ushered Shirley into the house. She was sure that the pilots would see her blonde hair and give away our hideout. The natives told us when the Japanese occupied Zamboanga. The feeling of being cut off and alone was never stronger. Although we were afraid of the Japanese, their reputation from the Nanking Massacre having preceded them, we also feared the Moros many of whom had a reputation for ruthlessness. The Japanese had freed many of the prisoners in the penal colony at San Ramon near Zamboanga, and some of these felons were roaming the hills looking for food.

From Daddy's writings:

> We observed the Japanese ships going north and south, sometimes singly and sometimes in convoy. The ships were all lit up at night. Apparently there was no enemy around to forestall them.

Early in our stay in Malayal, my father made a trip by land into Zamboanga. His mission was to get school books, check on the mission, and try to get some money. On his return, he was passing through Labuan, the halfway point, when he came upon a band of Moros having themselves a wild time bathing in a river. He writes:

> I really didn't know just what the reaction from them would be. But I was amazed when I heard someone say, "Oh, it's Mr. Mattocks from Zamboanga!" Some of our school boys in the group recognized me and came right over and welcomed me to the group. So we were thankful in many ways for the contact we had had with the people and the foundation of friendship that we had built through all the years. It served us in very good stead.

Weather and natural catastrophes were always something with which to be reckoned. There were several tremendous earthquakes. All the tubs containing rainwater on our back porch were toppled over by the shaking. At other times there were typhoons that caused rain for days. Mud from the ensuing mudslides blocked the trail to our water supply. There were times of terrific wind when the nipa siding on the shack blew off and had to be replaced. Our friends in the Glen were well-protected, situated as they were under a canopy of huge trees and surrounded by a high ridge.

Besides the whims of nature, about which we were powerless to do anything, were the wild animals that inhabited the forest around us. The one that we feared the most was the snake. Poisonous snakes were abundant. Several times, snakes attempted to get into the chicken house underneath our sleeping quarters. The hens, roosters, and ducks would set up fearsome squawking. We were, of course, awakened and would rush out of the house to assess the situation. One time, there was a seven-foot long tawny-colored snake stretched across the doorway to the hen house. Before my father could get something to do away with it, it slithered under the bamboo slats, which formed our flooring. We did not sleep well that night or for several nights thereafter. Thankfully, the chickens and ducks gave us warning when these and other predators entered the domain that was our common abode.

About June of 1942, the Handels decided to leave the mountains and take their luck with the Japanese. Mrs. Handel, particularly, found the life in the jungle trying. They thought, at that point, that their German passports would be looked upon favorably by the Japanese, and that the red "J" would not be recognized by the authorities. They were correct. They never gave our position away by divulging where they had been hiding. We didn't see them again until the end of our internment when they came to the front gate of Santo Tomas and gave us some eggs. The Filipina girls left about that time as well. After having made some contacts in Zamboanga, they felt it would be safe to return to their families. We were now just five and felt rather vulnerable and alone.

FINAL DAYS IN HIDING

Toward the end of 1942, our supplies began to give out; and it became more difficult to get goods at the Chinese store. Always, the Subanos were generous with their fruits and vegetables that we needed to supplant our own produce. But canned milk and other staples were not to be had. There were rumors of bands of marauders roaming the mountains, plundering villages, and stealing food. We felt more vulnerable since the departure of the Handels and the Filipinas.

In January 1943, we received word from the Japanese that all the hide-outs in the Malayal area should report to Zamboanga to surrender. It wasn't going to be easy to comply with the order without transportation. Daddy, Mr. Gulbranson, and Mr. Loptson, it was decided, would make the trip by vinta to Zamboanga and represent the larger group to the authorities. Two men from Forest Glen would come up to Cogon Cottage to stay with us while they were gone. A tremendous typhoon arose.

From my diary:

> January 11...Victoriano comes up with a note to Mr. Gulbranson (from the Japanese) commanding us to go to Zamboanga at once. Daddy goes to Forest Glen to have a meeting. Typhoon wind all night.

> January 12...Daddy comes back soaking wet and says he has to go to Zamboanga with Mr. Gulbranson and Mr. Loptson. They'll go by night because of the tribes in Labuan. But (later) Victoriano comes up with a note saying that the waves are too high. Vinta can't travel. Wait until further notice.

> January 13...Last night was the worst wind we ever had. I couldn't go to sleep a bit. Maybe God does not want us to go.

> January 14...Heard wild pigs in the camote field. Had Sunday School in the bodega. I think the Japanese will come for us any time. Saw eight Japanese planes.

> January 15...Victoriano comes up saying Daddy has to go tomorrow to San Ramon or Zamboanga. Another storm is coming over the mountain. The idea is that the Japanese might land on the shore during the night.

After the storm abated, the appointed men attempted another trip to Zamboanga.

January 19...Samsun came for his money. We ask Samsun to cargadore Daddy's things to the shores of Malayal to Ansagan's (the pastor) house. The duck laid an egg.

January 20...Before breakfast, Geoffrey and I went to the woods to get palms for the duck's nest. They like dark places. Up comes Daddy. He said that as they were about to leave for the shore five native soldiers (probably self-styled guerillas or bandits) armed with blunderbusses threatened them and kept them from going.

Just as they were about to depart down the banks of the Salupit River, the men found themselves facing five armed guerillas, who claimed to be part of the resistance force. The men were told not to report to the Japanese or great harm would befall those of us who were left behind. At this point, plans for surrender were aborted. We had the Japanese's order on one hand. On the other hand, we were threatened with facing harm from the local group of bandits. It was a very jittery time for all of us and much of the placid and serene, though primitive, life we had "enjoyed" for the year was now overshadowed by uncertainty and fear. Many rumors of what had happened to others hiding out on other islands had reached us. After the war, we found out that there had been wholesale annihilations of some of these groups. We had no idea where the other foreign nationals who had lived in Zamboanga were. We were right back to the first days of the war in terms of anxiety about the future.

From my diary:

January 23...Yesterday we saw warships at sea. Heard airplanes. We read, *Julius Caesar*. Dodong came with 313 olive-shaped tomatoes. Very silent. My! how silent everything is here.

January 25...Heard planes. Saw lots of warships.

January 27...We play games with the Clingens. Then they left. We saw where Malajo's kaingen is burned. We got three legs of venison. Indian came over and told us some Subano laws. Mr. Snead comes running up from Forest Glen and tells us that Japanese soldiers from Zamboanga are on the shore in Malalyal—one hundred of them.

The days of living in limbo were about to end. Mr. Snead's message terrified us. He did not linger, but turned around immediately and ran the two kilometers down the trail back to the Glen to prepare for whatever they faced in the next few hours.

Out came the emergency suitcases into which we crammed the remains of our worn out clothing. We prayed for deliverance. In no time, the Subanos were at the door. We gave them the dogs, frying pans and other utensils. Amban received the alarm clock. A toolbox was given to Agripino. We children said good-bye to the chickens and ducks as we gave them away to the Subano children. We waited. Suddenly, Mother looked up and saw two maps of the South Pacific nailed to the wall. If the Japanese came into the house, these would certainly cause trouble. She burned them at the stove. Mother cooked what little food was left; and we shared one last jar of marmalade although, in truth, we were too nervous to eat. We waited and waited. Nightfall came and there was no further word from the Glen. We tried to sleep fully dressed, expecting a troop of soldiers to barge in at any moment. It began to pour, but cleared up towards morning.

A short time after dawn, we saw smoke rising from the vicinity of Forest Glen. A Subano came running up the trail. "The Japanese have burned the camps and have taken all the people away!" he shouted, out of breath from his run.

What to do now? We were really alone now—a family of five in the wilds and jungles of Mindanao. I recall that there wasn't much choice about the next step. We had no arms, little food, no medicine. We might be putting the local population at risk.

We hoisted what we could on our backs and started our trudge down the mountains sinking in muck and mud with every step. We had no plan nor even an idea of what the next hour would bring.

From Daddy's writings:

And so, the Japanese came. They went to the American camp down below and we saw smoke rising from the valley. We wondered what in the world they were doing, whether they were acting as they had acted in various other places. We kept on packing what we could carry ourselves. This time there would be no one but ourselves to bear the burdens. We filled bottles of water. We started off, not with coconuts around our necks, but with our rattan suitcases, bedrolls and boiled water. We pushed our way through the muck and tall grass down to the beach below.

We continued along the shore to Kau-ah's tienda. Kau-ah felt that the Japanese had not known about us, or at least had not taken a count of those they did capture. He offered his upstairs front verandah as a place to sleep while we could arrange for a boatman to take us to San Ramon Penal Colony. We felt that would be the best place to turn ourselves in. We were relieved to be upstairs. A couple of months before, there had been a murder at the store right on the ample wooden counter. It probably wouldn't have worried Mother a bit to be downstairs, but I could not put the fact of the murder out of my mind.

We then went to the pastor's house to retrieve Daddy's kit bag that he had left there the previous week. We discovered that the house had been burned to the ground by the Japanese soldiers in retaliation for Ansagan's refusal to disclose the whereabouts of the Americans. What little Daddy had was even less now. We sifted through the ashes. All that remained: his small silver box for communion wafers glistened in the rubble.

While waiting for someone who was willing to ferry us down the coast, we washed our clothes in the nearby Malayal River. We worried about whether the Japanese would come back for us once they discovered they were missing a few. Being angry for the extra trip, would they then resort to cruel punishment? The Subanos' recounting of what had happened at Forest Glen did not allay our fears. The capturing group was led by some local men, now soldiers in the Japanese army. Before the war, a couple of them had been in prison for serious offenses. They were now in charge of rounding up Americans and other enemy nationals who were still hiding out.

We were told that the Forest Glen people were given an hour to pack up. That accomplished, hand grenades were then thrown into the encampment, and the place was set on fire. Within minutes the spot, which had been a haven for the past year, was in ashes. One of the soldiers himself hurled precious cans of evaporated milk down the river. The group then had to make its way down the slippery rocks to the shore. Among them was a cripple, an older couple, and the Hesses' new baby. No one seemed to know where they were all taken, but we assumed it would be Zamboanga City.

Kau-ah fed us for two days. At night we were kept awake by the slapping down of tiles during the all-night Mah-jong games. Finally, my parents were able to persuade Eusabio, a fisherman, that our presence was a menace to the Malayal community, and he agreed to borrow his uncle's banca to sail us as far as San Ramon. Daddy made one quick trip up to Cogon Cottage, but found the place pretty well ransacked.

As we assembled on the shore ready to climb into the banca, we noticed that many of the Subanos who had come to bid us farewell were wearing what few things we had left behind. Better them than the enemy, and it was small payment for all the shelter and comfort we had been given during our sojourn among them.

Mother gave Kau-ah a small box that contained a camera, a little jewelry, and a few valuables to hold for safekeeping. She also left a larger suitcase with kitchen utensils, some towels, and other household items. Amazingly, after the war, the box with the valuables was returned to our church headquarters in New York City. Nothing was missing.

We were ready to depart. At that moment, however, a tall Mestizo was holding forth with a crowd of Subanos around him. In his hand was a document that he was reading to the group. A bounty of five thousand pesos was being offered for the head of any American or British who could be turned in dead or alive. There was lots of murmuring among the assembled, and the bearer gave us a knowing smirk. After all, we had known him before the war.

Well, the banca was waiting, and we lost no time in hanging around while the natives discussed the document. Fortunately, none of those gathered seemed interested in collecting the prize. They shouted well wishes instead.

From Mother's writings:

> Kau-ah himself shouted, "Sun hong" meaning, obey the wind, the Chinese equivalent of Bon Voyage.

(1) Albert Klestadt, *The Sea Was Kind* (Singapore: Kangaroo Press, Pty., Ltd., 1959, 1988), p.120.

Eusabio had managed to find another boatman so there were now seven of us crammed into the little banca. We waved good-bye to the friends on the shore who had welcomed and sustained us; to the mountains that had given us refuge; to Lanote Creek that had given us water; and to a life, while primitive, and at times harsh, had taught us that as a family, we could pull together. We had survived under conditions we could not have imagined the year before. We set off, filled with thankfulness for our mountain existence, but filled with apprehension of what the next few hours would bring.

As usual, it began to rain, first with a drizzle and then a downpour. Without any covering, we became soaked to the skin. Mother had brought a couple of bananas that we all shared. None of us said anything. The sounds of the flapping sail, the waves slapping against the side of the boat, and the splashing of the rain were the only sounds. The boatmen said nothing, but kept eyes out for patrol boats or other signs that we might be discovered and that they would be implicated in our hideout and subsequent departure. Despite the warmth of the tropics we were all shivering, partly from being wet from the rain, but also out of intense fear.

When we were within a half a kilometer from San Ramon, Eusabio pulled over to the beach and let us out to walk the rest of the way along the rocky shore to the penal colony. The boatmen quickly turned the banca around and disappeared into the mist.

We picked up our bags and sopping bedrolls and trudged up the beach to the main house of the colony. We walked up onto the red-tiled verandah where some Japanese soldiers were sitting around at low tables playing mah-jong. We stood at a fair distance from them. They all had shaved heads and wore white loose fitting karate-like garments; not at all like the soldiers we had pictured. They glanced up, said nothing, and then went back to their game. We were slightly relieved at this first reception although we were all still tense.

In a few moments, a young Filipino dressed in what looked like a cast-off US Army uniform appeared. He whispered, "God Bless America" and was out of sight in a second. Another similarly dressed Filipino came by and gave us the "V" for victory sign, out of sight of the game players. Presently, this last man returned with a few pieces of chicken wrapped in a banana leaf and five cups of hot tea. We were a sight, the five of us, standing soaking wet with an ever-enlarging puddle around our feet. We were still in the very spot where we had first stepped onto the porch. With this offering of food and drink, we felt somewhat revived. It had been several hours since we had had the banana lunch.

After what seemed like an eternity, there appeared around the corner a tall, fierce-looking bearded military man, who from Kau-ah's description we knew to be the man who had led the expedition to the mountains three days previously. Our fears, which for a few fleeting moments had been somewhat allayed, now took control of us. We never saw a more fearsome man. On his uniform were many medals and insignia of the Japanese army. Previous to the war, this man had allegedly been serving time for serious crimes. He was released from prison when the invading troops came in and was given the responsibility of rounding up foreign nationals as well as other sympathizers to the U.S.

"Who are you and where are you from?" He bellowed.

My parents gave him the proper answers.

"Why did you run away from the camp when you knew we were coming?" He screamed.

Again the correct answers were given. They told him how we tried to surrender and that our plans had been thwarted. They also said that my father's clothes had been burned in the pastor's house; clothes that had been left in preparation for the trip to turn us in. He then yelled at us to follow him into his office, a bare bones cement cubicle down a long hallway.

A Filipino couple was standing near his desk looking clearly terrified.

"Remember," he shouted at the couple, "If I find any evidence that you are lying I will have you shot!"

From my father's writings:

> We were just basking in this unfamiliar hospitality after the offering of the chicken and tea, when suddenly at the end of the porch came on this fierce, cruel looking white man. [He was of mixed Spanish blood.] He had a pistol in his belt. He came charging through the Japanese officers and even they wondered why he was so angry. I told him that we tried to surrender, but couldn't.
>
> "No sir, we did not try to run away, we waited for you but you never came," I said fearfully. I could see that we were at the mercy of a fanatic and perhaps a sadist of the worst kind. He then gave a recital of how many people he had killed.

After this introduction, we five sat down in his office and the interrogation continued. We were still drenched to the skin but were so frightened by this man that we no longer felt wet. My parents seemed to answer his questions to his satisfaction. It was a bit tricky, as we did not want to give away the names of the people who had harbored us. His yelling abated abruptly. He said we were to stay in one of the bungalows usually occupied by a prison official. We were shown the cottage, a one-room sparsely furnished affair. At once we began to hang our belongings out to dry. I remember Mother stringing soaking wet toilet paper across everything.

A little later, the soldier returned and announced that he was taking the three of us children to his house for dinner. At dinner, we children were again given the third degree. I was quite circumspect with my answers but Geoffrey, being only seven years old, was most anxious to comply. A few kicks under the table put a silence to that. The soldier's children were nice looking and well behaved. One of them was an accomplished musician. The routine of the children having dinner with this family continued for four nights.

Despite the frightening introduction on the day of our arrival, we looked forward to playing with the children. Otherwise, we were confined to the little bungalow. Meanwhile, Mother and Daddy were not allowed to leave the cottage at all.

From my father's writings:

> The officer returned. In an about face he said, "I am your friend!"
>
> "Well," I said, "I certainly need a friend about now."
>
> He said, "Yes, and now I will take your three children."
>
> So he took the three children. Mrs. Mattocks and I sat in the cottage with the doors locked and windows barred. From time to time, the Japanese would come and look at us through the bars. After a while two Filipino prisoners came in with a tray of food and set it down in front of us. We were surprised to see fried bananas and some rice. None of us spoke because we didn't know if they were friend or foe. Then one of the prisoners whispered to me that the Americans were in Guadalcanal.

From Mother's writings:

> It was an agonizing two hours when the officer had the children. But to our intense relief his car tore up the driveway and the three hopped out and quite thrilled at their first auto ride in fourteen months. Then the soldier sank into a rattan chair and entertained himself (chiefly) with hair-raising tales of his days of Bataan fighting and his own kindness to the recently captured Americans. About two A.M. three heavy trucks arrived. His black eyes flashed.
>
> "Searching squad," he said.
>
> "Must go see what they've got." He was off.

On the fifth day, soldiers arrived. We were going to be taken to Zamboanga City and were excited by the prospect of joining the Forest Glen group although we weren't sure that that was where they were. We were herded into an open truck with a lot of Japanese soldiers. It was pouring rain. We got our first view of Zamboanga from the speeding truck. I was struck by the number of check points and Japanese sentries everywhere. The truck drew up in front of the Philippine Constabulary Barracks right across the field from our house. We were overjoyed to see the Forest Glen people on the porch and they welcomed us warmly. However, they whispered to us that we would be searched and any written materials, pencils or pens would be confiscated. They had been searched and even their Bibles had been taken. We didn't have much, but we quickly hid what we had.

From my diary:

February 2...Ate at the officer's house. A Japanese soldier told us that a truck was coming for us at twelve and to be ready. So we packed. Carmen interpreted for him. Twelve o'clock and the truck hasn't come yet. It's raining, of course. We play games with the children. Truck comes. There were many soldiers on it. It went so fast, I was dizzy. We arrive at Zamboanga. St. John's School and St. Alban's school were burned. It looked so different. The camp is at the Philippine Constabulary Barracks. The Forest Glen people are here.

February 3...Our house is across the street So near and yet so far. We cleaned the cubbyhole that we were supposed to have. Mother washed out our things. They're all wet again. We have to dry the toilet paper all over again.

February 4...The grown ups have a meeting to parcel out the jobs. My job is to wash dishes. (The coconut shells, that is.)

We quickly settled into a routine here. A meeting of the adults was held and the duties were parceled out. Across the field, we had a clear view of our old house. The Japanese Commandant had commandeered the property for himself.

The yard was a mess and some of our furniture was strewn about. We could see the bedposts still sticking up at the windows. We asked our guard, Mr. Iguchi, about going there and he said, "Even Japanese no go there."

Miss Suarez, one of the mission hospital nurses, told us that she had paid a courtesy call on the Commandant to get the lay of the land. She told us that we would not want to see the inside of the house. She reported that on our dining table, there was a coconut oil lamp burning. From this flame the soldiers lit their cigarettes. The paper they used to get the flame was torn from prayer books, Bibles and other books from my parents' collection.

When we first moved to Zamboanga, Mother had hired a Japanese carpenter to do some cabinetry work in the kitchen. Well, we were to find out that in addition to his carpentry skills, some wiring was installed which would be useful when the invasion was completed. This carpenter, it turned out, had military rank when the Japanese took over.

Our guard, Mr. Iguchi, was an elderly Japanese man who was given the duty of keeping us in check. Mother's writings give a good indication of what a kind man he was:

> This elderly man was one of the few bright spots among the hundreds to whose whims we were subjected the next two years. He managed trips to the market, the dentist, the hospital for us; he inveigled navy officials to let all sorts of food come in. On several occasions, he donated his daily sugar ration. He even wrangled the return of all the confiscated stationery and books. As a peaceful plantation owner, thirty years in the Philippines, he saw no reason for upsetting the status quo, and frankly said so. When upbraided for leaving us unwatched he defended himself: "These are good people, they will not run away. I know many of them now already many years." For all that, he was wily enough to warn us when to be alert.

From my diary:

February 19...Mr. Iguchi gave us some marbles. Seven each. Now the gang starts rolling marbles. I am sick. Mr. Iguchi, Mummy and I go to the hospital. We see Mrs. Enriquez, Joy and Jewel (friends from prewar). Miss Suarez and Mrs. Perez gave me some shells.

February 21...I went to the hospital. Saw Remy, Doctor Trota and a few nurses. Later I played with my seven marbles.

I was thrilled to see Remy again although I could not play with her. At one point, Dr. Trota slipped my father some money.

From my father's writings:

After a while, the Japanese allowed us to go to the hospital, Brent Hospital. I remember Dr. Trota wanting to see me especially, so I went in the sick parade. Dr. Trota took me away privately and asked the Japanese guard to step out of the room while he examined me. He told me how the Japanese were wrecking the hospital and the awful things that were happening there. Dr. Trota passed me thirty pesos. He told me how the commanding officer was using our house there on the waterfront for his headquarters.

To everyone's surprise, Kau-ah appeared on the doorstep one day carrying a couple of our suitcases that had been left behind in his care. Anxiously, they were opened, as we were hopeful that they were the ones that contained clothing. The only thing left inside was a meat grinder, an eggbeater and an empty flashlight. Kau-ah was very apologetic, but he said that he had been looted twice by bandits on the way down.

From my diary:

....Kau-ah brings some of our things from Malayal. Bandits ransacked everything. Practically nothing left...

"o." They took our things, the robbers! Mummy and I went to Brent Hospital with the guard. The nurses gave us some food.

From Mother's writings:

We were deeply sensible of the risk the Chinese merchant had undertaken, and that bidding our friend good-bye meant the last break with a fairly free and happy, though hard life.

After a month in Zamboanga where we felt relatively comfortable, surrounded as we were by loyal and loving people and a guard who tried to make things easier, we were told one day by the military that we were being moved. They didn't say where but to pack up, just to "chop, chop, hully, hully." It didn't take us long to get our meager belongings together. That done, we were told to untie everything for an inspection...a routine that was to be repeated many times in the next two years. We stood on the porch, waiting for the trucks to take us to the pier. Our band of thirty-seven waited for the next chapter to unfold. It was February 1943.

From my diary:

February 25...Today's the day. Soldiers come. Davao, the dread. We packed up and were taken to the dock. Good-bye Zambo. We got on a transport and were put in the hold of the ship with about three hundred Japanese soldiers. SMELL! FILTH! OH! Garbage and offal were dumped in the center of the hold.

TRANSPORT #760

Once aboard the rusty hulk of the transport/troop ship #760, we were lined up on deck and counted The ship had sustained damage in some sea battle; a huge gash scarred its side. On board were several hundred Japanese soldiers, many of whom were wounded.

It didn't take long to count the thirty-seven of us, and we were soon ushered down into the hold of the ship. We shared the space with many of the soldiers. Garbage and trash were piled up in the center of the hold. Some of this was shoved aside to make space for our baggage, such as it was. The stench was horrendous. The soldiers didn't seem to mind, but it was very offensive to us.

Around the walls of the hold were shelf-like compartments that served as the sleeping quarters. We had to stoop to crawl into the lower shelves or hoist ourselves up to get into the upper ones. Our group was assigned a small section while the soldiers occupied the rest. Lining the floor of the shelves were filthy straw mats. It appeared that the bulky and dirty cork life preservers were to serve as pillows. No other bedding was needed as the temperature in the hold must have been close to one hundred degrees.

It took a few minutes to adjust to the darkness and the smell. The top of the hatch was closed, save for a small slit which allowed a bit of filtered sunlight to enter as well as a suggestion of badly needed fresh air.

The ship set sail down through the Celebes Sea soon after we boarded. We were told that our destination was Davao on the eastern coast of Mindanao. At Parang some soldiers who were dressed for battle as well as the wounded, carried on stretchers, disembarked.

We were allowed up on the deck at times during the daylight where twice daily we were served rice and a sort of soybean mash. All around us, the soldiers were enjoying the contents of Red Cross comfort kits intended for prisoners of war, both civilian and military. A few of the soldiers were friendly with the children when the officers were out of sight. We were given a can of Hershey's cocoa from one man. A soldier gave me a fat red pencil that I kept for most of the war. We were all in the wretched hold together: captors and captives.

From my diary:

February 26...Today the soldiers in the hold are kind to us children. They gave us candy and bananas. Rice and stew is our food for every meal.

From Mother's writings:

We eyed enviously cases of evaporated milk slopped extravagantly over the decks. The Captain's huge police dog, cared for by a soldier in the compartment next to ours, consumed enough corned beef for a battalion. The ship's clinic revealed medical supplies of the best American brands.

After a three-day voyage, we arrived at Davao Harbor where the captain anchored. Gathered on deck, under a blistering sun, an interminable wait to disembark tested our fortitude. We waited for lighters that eventually drew up alongside the ship to ferry us to the docks. The baggage was then heaved over the side into the lighters below. A rope ladder was slung over the railing of the ship and one by one we gingerly edged our way down the swaying rungs to the waiting boat. The swells in the harbor rocked the lighter making it difficult to step feet-first into the boat. For the children and the nimble this was accomplished without incident. However, some of our group required a great deal of assistance in negotiating this exit from the ship. The men of our group were ordered to unload the lighters that contained not only our baggage, but that of the soldiers disembarking at this port. Sadly, we saw many American prisoners of war, gaunt and threadbare, doing heavy work around the docks. Our guard told us not to make eye contact with them. We wondered if some of our good officer friends from Pettit Barracks in Zamboanga were among them.

Once the bedrolls and baggage were loaded, we piled into an open truck and were driven at breakneck speed to the banks of the Davao River. A once-substantial bridge across the river lay in twisted ruins. The banks of the river were mucky, steep, and difficult to navigate. Mr. Davis of our group who was in his seventies couldn't manage to carry his suitcase. As he was being helped by another internee a soldier from behind grunted:

"He take!" the soldier said, pointing to Mr. Davis.

"But he's old and he's been sick," the internee said.

"Never mind, old, young, sick, well, all work now in New Era!" the soldier barked.

Mr. Davis was forced to crawl on all fours down to the river's edge. Once assembled, we were ferried across the river in bancas. Filled with apprehension, we picked up our belongings and set out along the dusty road.

From my diary:

February 28...Early in the morning we arrive at Davao. We had to wait a long time before we could get on the lighters and get off the boat. The soldiers just threw all our things in the lighters. When we finally got ashore we were counted. Thirty-seven in all. The Japanese made us stand in the hot sun a long time. Finally a truck came and took us to the river. We had to unload our things again and get into little boats. When we got to the other shore, we unloaded our things again and then had to walk a long way.

8 HAPPY LIFE BLUES

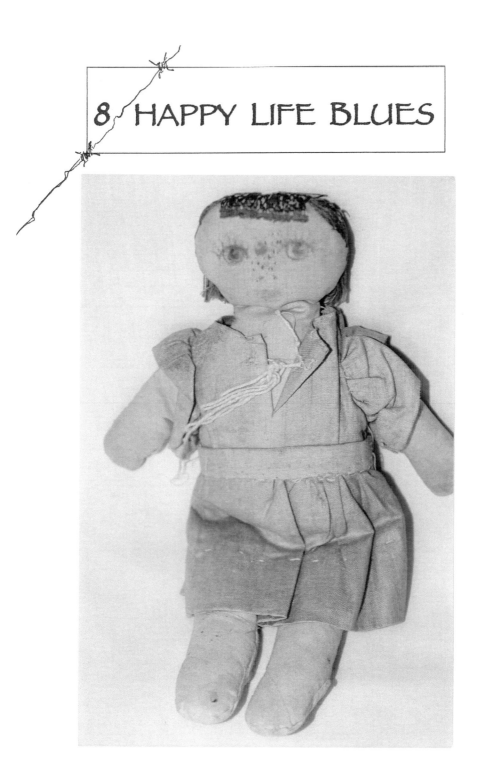

Our group from Zamboanga joined the two hundred and fifty or so internees already settled into life at an old cabaret a couple of kilometers out of Davao City at a place called Matina. Who were they?

From Mother's writings:

> We were a composite group of sojourners in a far off land,-miners, engineers, planters, nurses, mechanics, and teachers. Our ages ranged from six months to eighty-one years; we were denizens of nearly a dozen countries; among us were veterans of the Spanish-American War who married Filipinas, and had not returned to the United States for these forty-three years.

> Many among the group were people like ourselves who had hidden in the mountains of Mindanao and had only recently been rounded up.

> We were greeted warmly and with looks of relief as we joined other members of our particular missionary group. We had lost contact with one another for over a year. Stories were exchanged about our months on the run.

> "Happy Life Blues" was the inscription on the plaque hanging askew over the entrance to the former run-down cabaret, now a prison camp. The first entrants to be imprisoned here adopted this moniker facetiously. In reality, however, it wasn't too far off the mark.

> The dance hall itself, a low-slung wooden structure with a galvanized tin roof, was set fairly well back from the dusty road which ran by the property. Other buildings on the grounds included some nipa shacks, and a fairly large nipa building that served as a kitchen shed, although most of the cooking was done in the open air. Away from the main house stood a large nipa and bamboo structure used as a school, a church, and a meeting place. Two small nipa and bamboo enclosures served

as shower stalls: one for females, the other for males. The guardhouse was situated at the front of the property at the entrance to the camp. A single electric wire stretched from a pole on the road across the grounds to the dance hall, the only structure with electricity, and unreliable at that. Barbed wired encircled the compound.

The first to be interned here months previously found the place practically uninhabitable. There were no facilities for bathing or cooking. The property was strewn with layers of trash. By the time we arrived at Happy Life Blues, the physical shape of the camp showed the results of a lot of hard work and innovation on the part of the first arrivals.

After preliminary greetings, our family was assigned to a space on the mezzanine floor together with the other families from Zamboanga. Our living space was delineated with chalk lines and two by fours; it measured about fifteen feet wide feet by ten feet deep. At the back area was a waist-high wall over which we could look down upon the sea of mosquito nets below. Many of the single men occupied the main floor.

At first, all we had were our bedrolls and tied-together belongings. Others who had preceded us had managed to build bamboo benches and cots. But that would come in time for us. Mosquito nets, rolled up during the day, were hung up on wires, which crisscrossed above the area. We unrolled the bedrolls at night and slept on the floor, which was none too clean. Before rolling the "beds" up in the morning, we conducted the daily ritual of picking the bedbugs out of the bedding. No matter how thoroughly we debugged, the infestation was rampant by evening. Many times we were bitten, and upon waking, we'd find ourselves covered with welts and bloody spots. At various times, cockroaches, scorpions, and spiders as well as the bedbugs shared our space. We were told that prior to our arrival, nests of cobras had to be cleared out from under the building.

The availability of water was a continual problem. There were only three outside cold-water taps for the entire camp. The flow was unreliable and often, it was turned off for hours at a time. When it was on, there was a rush to gather enough to wash the dishes, the clothes, or to drink. Despite the heat, we wore our clothes for days, partly because of the water shortage, and partly to save the fraying fabric. Only two or three at a time could fit into the women's shower cubicle. Water came out of the one showerhead in spurts or a few drips at a time. We had to be quick about bathing. A line always formed when the news went out that the water was on. Without warning, the flow would cease, usually when one was "soaped" up. Soap was at a premium, and we used every sliver we could salvage. None was ever left in the shower area for someone else to use.

Most of the girls wore shorts and a shirt; the women, skirts or shorts; and the boys and men usually dressed in shorts only. After a few months there were many interesting patch jobs on all our clothing. For shoes, we wore wooden bakyas, since the leather shoes we had at the beginning of the war we had long since outgrown, even with the toes cut out. Some of the men made sandals out of old rubber tires and had created quite a shoe business at which they either made the sandals or repaired the bakyas. Foot protection was essential, as the ground was rife with all sorts of parasitic creatures. We had no rain gear; and when the tropical deluges descended, we just got soaked. At times, the cool rainwater refreshed us.

The toilet facilities were of the crudest sort. Elongated outhouses were built at a distance from the cabaret. The women's outhouse was an enclosed structure made of nipa, wood and bamboo. The "seats" were several holes cut in a long plank (no privacy here, either). The pit was full of maggots, flies, and other vermin. Some people had a stash of toilet paper; others just grabbed banana or other leaves on the way out. Sometimes, old newspaper was meted out. When one latrine became full, it was filled in and another trench was dug a bit further out. Having to go to the "benjo" (Japanese word for toilet) at night was a daunting experience. I was petrified to leave the building after dark. People kept chamber pots or buckets in their quarters and, of course, in the morning someone had the emptying duty. However, if one were brave enough to make the trek to the benjo in the dark of night, it was necessary to chant "benjo, benjo, benjo" all the way out. Failure to do this or answer to the guard's shouting of "tomaru" (halt) meant the risk of getting a bayonet in the ribs!

Privacy was a lost commodity. There was no place to escape the crowded conditions. Babies crying at night would elicit shouts of "shut up" (and worse) from every corner. Other night sounds would raise the ire of some sleepless internee. Sometimes the Japanese guards, particularly the Kempeitai (military police), would come stalking down the aisle in the middle of the night. One was wakened by the stomp of the boots and the clank of the sabers as the police made their way through the maze of mosquito nets. Since we were sleeping on the floor, one misstep by these soldiers meant that we might have a boot in the face.

One particular set of brothers who lived in Davao before the war had built a shanty next to the barbed wire fence. Some of the locals in the barrio outside would sneak tuba (a native drink made from fermented coconut tree sap) to them. After these men had quaffed more than enough, they would steal the tire rim and iron rod that were used to rouse the camp from sleep or to announce roll call or meals. They would march through the building banging the rim and waking everyone up. Lying on our mattresses on the floor, we wondered when one of the inebriated would come crashing down. I never heard of anything happening to them, although our chairman probably reprimanded them.

Internally, an elected committee ran the camp. J. Franklin Ewing, S.J., was our chairman. Any connection with the guards or the authorities was to go through the committee via the interpreters. Two missionaries who had lived in Japan previously and were fluent in Japanese were the liaisons with the captors. One of the interpreters, Mr. Cary, had lived in Davao and knew some of the local guards. Being an interpreter was difficult. Out of necessity, a great deal of time had to be spent with the guards as well as the Kempeitai. Disgruntled internees would suspect the interpreters of some sort of fraternization with the enemy. It was a thankless job, and most of us were grateful that we had spokespeople who could at least explain our needs to the authorities, and, conversely, could translate what the Japanese orders meant for us.

It was essential that this disparate group of individuals living in such close quarters under adverse conditions have some framework by which to live. There were disagreements and complaints. It was best to settle them under camp rules imposed and voted on by the majority than go complaining to the Japanese.

Cleanliness and freedom from tropical diseases and epidemics were on the minds of those entrusted with sanitation responsibilities. Shortages of water, soap, and disinfectants made it difficult to keep the environs clean. There was no doctor among the internees. Fortunately, there were no major outbreaks of disease. A clinic was run each morning where sores were dressed and aspirin dispensed. For more serious matters, a detail went into town occasionally, and the local doctor or doctora tended to the sick. I remember reading that those trips took place on Mondays, and I am not sure what happened if one needed attention the other days. On occasion, the doctor did come out to the camp after being summoned.

One of the elected positions in camp was Entertainment Chairman. My father was elected to that post. He was a good choice, since he was a bit of an actor himself. He had a wonderful sense of humor, a trait that under those conditions could carry one a long way. Entertainment was of a grassroots, homespun type. A men's and women's chorus was formed. All the renditions were a cappella since no one had a musical instrument. The children participated in little plays or memorized and recited poems. Sometimes there were skits with overtones of our plight. We tried to make light of hunger, bare feet, bedbugs, lack of water, and benjo problems. We had no reliable news of how the war was going. If internees on a detail were going to town to pick up rice or other foodstuffs, they might see a newspaper, fleetingly. Reading between the lines was an art form in trying to find the truth in the Japanese news reports. Years ago, I wrote this description of our Saturday night entertainment:

Smiles at Happy Life Blues

Saturday evening was entertainment night at the bedbug, cockroach-infested cabaret that was home to us in Davao. Poetry recitations, skits and shaky renditions of old favorite musical numbers were the offerings performed outside on the steps of the dance hall, our makeshift stage.

The guards were recruits from the local Davao Japanese

population. They squatted around the periphery of gathered internees ready to relieve the ennui of their assignment.

With a bit of temerity we began by standing and singing the National Anthem. We concealed amusement as we watched the guards stand also. After a couple of shows, they appeared to be humming along. The high point of our week came to an abrupt end one Saturday evening when Tanaka San, the Kempeitai Commandant, made an unexpected appearance. Recognizing the tune and its implications instantly, he severely admonished the guards, and threatened to close the show forever.

The memory of those few moments of seeing our guards rise to honor the enemy brought smiles to our faces for the duration.

◆

In prewar times, Davao had the largest Japanese population outside of Japan. Many of our guards were drawn from the locals. It was lowly duty for the Japanese to guard a group of white "colonists." No wonder they enjoyed our entertainment which included baseball games in addition to the aforementioned shows. Sometimes they would join in the games. But when Tanaka San came around, the fun was off. He conducted regular inspections of our belongings, commandeering anything that took his fancy, including one of my diaries.

Roll call was a twice-daily ritual, rain or shine. The great tire rim gong would be banged with the iron rod, a call to assemble on the front plaza; men and boys on one side and women and girls on the other. We were counted by a guard or a member of the Kempeitai and were required to stand by fives. However, there were seventy-eight females so there was a line lacking two people. By the guard's estimation there should have been five in every row. There was always much yelling, grunting and screaming about this lack of five people in one row. Patiently, the interpreter would try to explain the mathematics of counting by fives. It always made for a lot of unnecessary standing and a lot of squirming children. Once in a while two already-counted people would jump into the odd line to save a scene. Little tricks pulled off like this gave us a laugh and the hope that maybe the Japanese wouldn't win the war after all.

From Mother's writings:

> One great solace these mornings [at roll call] was the beautiful cone of Mount Apo, reflecting in her lofty mists the roseate hues of early dawn. "I will lift up mine eyes unto the hills," (our oft repeated psalm.)

Mount Apo was a large volcano which loomed in the background of the camp. In 1945, I wrote of impressions I had of that time:

Apo

Ichi, ni, san, si!
My eyes followed the arrogant guard as he droned on in the counting of the next row of prisoners. An unusual light attracted my attention. The delicate sunrise surrounding Mount Apo (the highest mountain the Philippines), whose name meant chief or head one, offered peace and contentment.

Apo was bold and stood erect and unafraid. A soft pearly veil of mist shyly crept upward while a scarf of pale pink turning red floated in, like worshipers throwing flowers upon a goddess. A thin blue line of smoke threaded its path toward heaven, giving a feeling of warmth and security.

Apo's colossal peaks and gigantic crags towered far above her other sisters and as Apollo drove his chariot higher into the sky, Apo shed her rose gown and donned her dress of gray. Her look of serenity overwhelmed me as I stood in the line in the dawn of another day as a captive.

◆

Food—the buying, growing, preparation, and serving of it took up most of the day for those internees assigned to those jobs. Basically, our meals consisted of some variation of rice. In the morning, the rice mush, which we called lugao, was sometimes served with coconut milk. Like our "milk" from the mountains, this was made from squeezing coconut gratings. Water was added to increase the supply. Once in a while we would be treated to a banana. Coffee was made from a combination of roasted corn and a few coffee beans. Most of the children drank the "coffee." Because it had been boiled, we considered it a safe beverage. For lunch, sometimes there would be a sort of stew we called "gulay." One could expect anything in the pot when gulay was on the menu. Once the Japanese sent in a ton of eggplant into the camp. There was no way this could be consumed before it rotted.

Meat was scarce and was obtained from the local slaughterhouse up the road. When the men came back with the wheelbarrows of "meat," it was usually just hoofs, heads, and tails. At least the evening meal of rice was sometimes augmented with a few shreds of beef. Sometimes they brought buckets of blood to be made into blood pudding. One of the nastiest jobs in camp was the scraping of the offal to get enough meat to add to the evening's stew. Hungry as I was at times, I could not bring myself to eat the blood pudding flaps that were served.

Mother's writing describes the procurement of meat:

> Six men returned with handcarts and assorted containers full of cows' heads and tails.....the next week it was hearts, liver and blood. As cattle became scarcer we were reduced to the further extremities of horns and hoofs, of which we had supposed glue to be a byproduct. However, we found nothing in the resulting stew that "stuck to our ribs."

Occasionally, there were peanuts. These were roasted and made into peanut butter. We used the meat grinder that was returned to us by Kau-ah (in Zamboanga) to grind the nuts. If we had a banana, we slit the banana lengthwise and spread peanut butter between the slices.

A sugar cane press had been procured. Once in a while when canes were brought into camp, they were pressed, and the resulting liquid was boiled and made into syrup. Sucking on a cane was something we children looked forward to.

There was no bread, butter, milk, or refrigeration of any sort. Our family, after standing in the chow line, would take its rations of food up to our quarters and eat at the bamboo table that my father had made. Cleaning up after the meal was a chore, as everyone jockeyed for the few drips of cold water that came from the taps.

From Mother's writings:

Meanwhile the be-all and end-all of life continued to be food. The only items furnished us were gravel-laden rice or grubby cracked corn and a small ration of salt. All else we paid for by assessment, chiefly with borrowed money...It is on record that we were continually refused the commonest accouterments-even when available.

We were told time and again that there were Red Cross comfort kits lying in bodegas and in piles at the docks in Davao City. We never received any in this camp. We were always buoyed up by rumors of Red Cross kits, only to be disappointed time and time again.

In addition to the cooks and food procurement, other jobs needed filling. Everyone who was able was assigned a job. The vegetable and rice cleaning was pretty much in the women's domain, while the heavier work and the details for food were assigned to the men. For the most part, the Roman Catholic priests assumed the teaching duties. There had been a great separation between the Roman Catholic priests and the Protestant missionaries before the war. Their paths seldom crossed. Now, having been herded all together, the schism became unimportant. We were all in this together. It was part of the great leveling experience. Survival depended upon working together, not liturgical differences.

One of the jobs assigned to those over ten years old was the gathering of palm fronds. Several of us that age and older would be called to meet in front of the cabaret in the morning after breakfast. With a guard, we would walk several kilometers up road to a swampy area where the palms grew. It is hard to believe, but we were given bolos to chop the branches down.

Then, of course, these fronds had to be dragged back to the camp along the dusty road under the blazing sun. The weaving of the palm leaves fell to the younger children and older ladies. If one had made the frond trip, then he or she was off the hook for weaving, although we all did help at times. Once woven, the fronds were used to side the little outbuildings or to patch up roofs. Sometimes the children were asked to go on other details.

From my diary:

> ....This morning Shirley and I went on a kangkong (better known as slippery greens) detail to the Matina River with several other children. We went past kilometer nine and didn't get much kangkong. On the way we jumped in the river with all our clothes on. The guard bought us fried bananas and a pomelo. On the way back we went in the river again. On arriving home we were tired. We had walked eleven kilometers.

Mother wasn't too happy about us jumping in the filthy, dirty river or eating fried bananas from a street vendor.

In addition to doing our share of the work, we attended school. The classes were held in the large nipa building that also served as a church. We were divided into two groups: junior and senior. I was in the latter. As mentioned previously, most of the teachers were the priests. We had little paper and few books. As a result, most of the work was done orally, sort of Socrates style, with the instructor holding forth and the pupils gathered around him. We had no desks, and for seats we dragged boxes or crates to the building each day. The senior classes were: Spanish, arithmetic, reading, music, writing, and history. I have a report card from those days written on the back of a hookworm report! During a particularly violent storm, the school blew down. Until it could be righted, we held classes under the trees! Midday there was always a siesta period. It was a welcome respite from the intense heat. We had no fans or cooling devices of any sort although sometimes a breeze wafted through the open windows on the mezzanine.

At age eleven, I was entrusted with an important task. Fr. Ewing, the camp chairman, approached my mother and asked if she would be willing to let me do a job for him. At that time, there were American submarines off the coast of Mindanao. Some were delivering arms to the resistance forces, and others were taking people on board who had managed to avoid being captured. This particular task which Fr. Ewing wanted help with entailed getting information from some of the internees about whom certain details were lacking. Names and addresses of next of kin were needed by the State Department. Some of the people I had to contact were those who had been in hiding for a period of time.

This "job" involved going around discreetly to avoid attracting any attention whatsoever. I would memorize a few names and addresses and then at an appropriate time deliver them to either Fr. Ewing or to the driver of a garbage truck. The driver must have memorized them also, for I don't remember any paper being used in the transactions. I had inadvertently left my own name off the list. When we arrived back in the States years later, anxious relatives inquired about me in the first mail we received. For my efforts in this endeavor I was given a celluloid doll. As I look back on it, it seems paradoxical that I was old enough to be entrusted to complete a sensitive task requiring utmost secrecy, and yet young enough to be thrilled at a gift of a doll.

As time went on, a few more people were brought into the camp from outlying areas. The cabaret became overcrowded. The Japanese then allowed those who had the means and skill to build shanties around the edge of the property. These weren't much more than a nipa roof and a bamboo floor raised off the ground. The sides were sawali, (woven bamboo strips). A few families took advantage of this for more privacy. As the shanties were occupied, more space was made available on the mezzanine floor.

The main interpreter of the camp, Frank Cary, shared a shanty with Walter Tong. Neither man had families interned in Davao. Mr. Cary's family was in the States and Mr. Tong's family was in Baguio on Luzon, where the children had been attending Brent School. Since the Tong children and we children were the same ages, Mr. Tong "adopted" us three. We didn't have a shanty, so we enjoyed the hospitality of the Cary-Tong shanty. It gave us a place to escape from the ward-like atmosphere of the main building.

In Frank Cary's book, *Letters from Internment, Davao and Manila*, he wrote:

> Yesterday, Mr. Tanaka came out to camp and asked the men from the British Isles whether they would like to return to England if an exchange ship could be arranged... One man married to an American wife has three interesting children. They (the wife and children) have dual citizenship. [A reference to our family, I believe.] A camp like this is fertile soil for rumours. Today we are a-humming with the chances of an exchange. I hope the negotiations go right through and that these folks can get away soon. (1)

There were several such "bones" like this thrown out during our internment. People fed on these rumors. They were fodder for much discussion and speculation.

Money was always a problem. Except for small rations of wormy rice and corn, we were expected to fend for ourselves. The Japanese allotted to each internee what was the equivalent of twelve and a half cents a day. Out of this, we were expected to pay not only for food, but also electricity, medicine, sanitation supplies, and, in fact, anything we needed for our existence.

I have read that the captors were usually in arrears with their payments. Sometimes there was aid from the Philippine Red Cross, or the International Red Cross. At times, those imprisoned who had funds, contributed to the good of the whole.

There was one small payment to the people of our mission from the mission in Manila. Otherwise, the "have-nots" borrowed from the "haves," and sometimes were charged exorbitant rates for doing so. Promissory notes were signed. After the war, when my father was back at St. Luke's in Manila, a woman from prison camp days looked him up to remind him that he owed her a miniscule amount of money. For what, he couldn't remember (neither could she), but he took her word for it and paid with interest.

To alleviate the boredom and routine of camp life, contests of various sorts were held from time to time. I wish I could recall the limerick, which won me first prize. My award was a tiny bar of Lux soap. At the time, this sliver of soap was coveted more than the honor of winning the contest.

Life dragged on in a fairly monotonous manner. Always at the forefront was the scavenging for food and the scratching out of gardens in the pitiful soil. Details of men were organized to go into town to pick up foodstuffs. Much of what they brought back was barely edible. Rice was filled with worms, pebbles, and bits of wire. Some of what they were allowed to get were scrapings off the bodega floor. Very few of the internees had lived in Davao before the war; there was little chance of offerings from friends on the outside.

I remember that some of the very old men in camp began to "lose it." They wandered about aimlessly muttering to themselves. At times they were incontinent. And it was not always the elderly. There was a young man of twenty-two who went stark-raving mad. He climbed up on a roof in the hot sun and had to be coaxed down. Finally, he was taken to some place of confinement in the city.

A few entries from my diary give a glimpse of everyday life:

....Cecily's birthday. Mr.Tong gave me a piece of soap and Arlene gave me a stick of sugar cane.

....I am not on vegetables today. Mother read us "Robinson Crusoe." I am very tired.

....Today men go for rations. Fr. Ewing went shouting through the building that people must not go out of the house because one of the guards is missing. Guards are excited. They order lights out.

....Story comes out. One guard, the squad leader, went to the Benjo. He disappeared and didn't come back. Tanaka San is here today.

There wasn't much variety in the meals. But when some concoction was especially appealing on the chow line, it might be praised in song. One that I remember is:

> Won't you bring back, won't you bring back
> Father Abbitt's chowder
> Every spoonful, makes a tuneful
> Makes you sing the louder.

Fr. Abbitt was one of our mission's priests who had kitchen duty. His job was to stir the rice in huge cawas (vats) with a wooden paddle. This usually required getting up at sunrise and standing over a hot smoky fire. He must have gotten innovative at one time; as a result, causing everyone in camp to rejoice at what we called "chowder."

We didn't know much about the progress of the war. Our thoughts were on day-to-day survival. We felt a certain safety in our numbers. Some people wallowed in depressing talk, but among the families there was a tone of optimism and a desire to make the best out of the situation. Recently, however, I came across a letter from my mother written on the occasion of my twelfth birthday. I realize now that she kept her fears well-hidden from us children.

My dear child, Margaret Cecily:

Twelve years ago tonight I had been in St. Luke's Hospital about twenty-four hours expecting you to make your appearance at any moment. When you finally arrived on the morning of the tenth you were brought into my room, beautiful, blue-eyed daughter...angel with pink skin and a fine head covered with terraces of tiny curls, a sight I shall never forget.

At eight o'clock your father came in with a bunch of roses for me and three little buds for you. For several years I kept one of them pressed, but it was lost before we left Manila. I love to think on those days, your early life in Santa Mesa, the birth of Shirley and the happiness you brought to all those you met in America and England, but especially to Grandpa Latham.

But we cannot go on living in the memories, thinking only of the past. The days whiz by as you yourself realize. We have to face them as they are. Four years ago today we landed at Newtonville on our way to Waltham. We learned that Grandpa had died on my birthday. Disappointment often enters suddenly into our lives and the sadness often returns though we may not speak of it to others. But there are other things which bring sadness and disappointment to us. These things can or cannot be under our control.

Now it brings tears to my eyes, this calm, balmy night to look on the setting moon and feel no control in this place. I wish you were here and that I could talk to you-say some words of cheer or love to make you realize what I want you to know.

You think me hard on you or that I expect so much of you, but you are capable of carrying much responsibility. After all, you are the eldest and you have had a better start than Shirley or Geoffrey. But I have cracked under the strain of this place. Life in the mountains was difficult, but we were all able to understand each other. In this place misunderstandings increase as we are all crowded together.

As a child, you have a right to expect some little gift. But I have nothing to give you. No present for my big, little girl. But I can give you love in the hope that it will help you hold up all the days of the imprisonment in camp and through the years. Remember your duty and your place in the family.

I have been very tired lately because of a heavy heart. All of us need to have understanding. Twelve years of Margaret Cecily have brought me joy.

With much love, your mother, Dorothy

As we neared Christmas of 1943, the children began to feel the excitement of the season even under those dire circumstances. There was talk of each boy and girl receiving a small gift. Men talented in woodcarving were whittling wooden toys for the boys. Some women were stringing squash seed bracelets for the girls. The camp carabao was going to be slaughtered as a celebration of real roast beef instead of heads and tails. For each other in the family, we copied poems or drew pictures.

While we were at roll call on the morning of December twenty-third, Tanaka himself appeared for the counting. He announced that we were going to be moved to another camp. For a while, there had been rumors that we were going to be transferred to Santo Tomas Internment Camp in Manila, but we had hoped that Christmas could be spent at Happy Life Blues.

Tanaka gave us two hours to pack up. "Speedo, speedo, hully, hully," he said. It's hard to believe, but even in a prison camp, one accumulates junk. We sorted and packed and were out in front at the appointed time. The men in the kitchen quickly cooked up the food that was left.

The pitiful assortment of our belongings was tied up with rattan and string. Tanaka appeared on the scene again and ordered everyone to open his bags for inspection. A cadre of guards appeared to do this job. Unfortunately, the Mattocks family got Tanaka himself who tore open the bundles we had so carefully assembled. He spied one of my diaries from the mountains and flipped through the scribblings, and then he took his bayonet to it. I guess I was lucky because diaries were forbidden, and my fate could have been worse. Mother thought he had destroyed it because of my having drawn the Japanese flag on the wings of a plane I had used in an illustration. In any case, he appropriated some other items and then told everyone to pack up again.

He then announced that we wouldn't be leaving until the next day. We were told to leave everything as it was. In an hour, a tropical deluge descended and all the baggage received the usual soaking. We went back into the building and spent a restless night on the bare wooden floors. Fortunately, some of the hastily cooked food was available.

Early the following day, the clanging of the gong roused us. We were ordered to appear at the front in a half hour. Since we were still dressed from the previous day and our belongings were already packed and on the plaza, this wasn't too hard.

Waiting for us were open army trucks. Our sopping wet baggage was thrown into the trucks, and we piled in after it. The sun had barely risen as we raced down the streets to the Taloma docks. Very few Filipinos observed our exodus. As we sped by, we saw emaciated, tattered, and gaunt-looking American prisoners of war working on an airfield.

At the docks was a string of three lighters, at the head of which was a tugboat. We piled in one of the little barges. The kitchen crew had quickly grabbed what food they could, but the Japanese helped themselves to it as soon as we got on board.

After being towed a few kilometers out into the harbor, we pulled up alongside the SS *Shinsei Maru #1*, a rusty hulk of a freighter converted into a troop ship. Someone said that the translation of the ship's name meant "Truly Flourishing." True or not, we soon found out that it was flourishing, all right. It was full of crawling vermin of all kinds.

Once alongside, a rope ladder was let down for us to climb up to the deck. This exercise was an impossible feat for the weak, lame, and little children. Finally, a sort of rope gangway was lowered and those unable to manage the ladder were able to board. Once on deck, we were counted and counted and counted. No one had jumped ship! After several hours in the blazing sun, we were shown our quarters in the hold.

SHINSEI MARU #1

It was December 24, 1943. Transport *Shinsei Maru #1* lay at anchor in Davao Bay. Her water line was high as she awaited cargo as well as the two hundred and eighty prisoners who were about to clamber aboard. On deck, the broiling tropical sun penetrated our bodies. While our guard, Tanaka San, counted and recounted us, we stood in roll call formation. The children were squirmy, and the older prisoners began to feel faint. We had not had food or water since the evening before. Once again, our fortitude was being tested. "The barbarians are soft," the captors told us time and again.

Roll call completed, we asked for our quarters, to escape the relentless sun.

"Oh yes, so solly, the Japanese army take all into consideration," we were told.

"Down there." They pointed to the cargo area.

Cautiously, we groped our way down a rusty companionway to the hold below. We were prodded from the rear by beast-like grunts. As soon as we got our bearings, we realized that we shared the cargo hold with piles of scrap iron, pieces of machinery, and material that could be used to make ammunition. A few rays of sunlight managed to escape into the area through the cracks of the covered hatch above.

As in Transport #760, the walls were lined with two tiers of shelves about three feet high. Six people were assigned to a compartment, which was lined with straw mats and heavy cork life preservers. We groped our way on all fours into a compartment. There was room to sit but not stand.

We lay there in this dark, sticky, claustrophobic environment for what seemed like hours. We humans were not alone. Soon it became apparent that we shared space with an army of ship's rats.

Sporadic screams soon gave way to wholesale crying out. We felt them crawling all over us, and random swatting in the dark did nothing to deter them. The hold was alive with screams, children crying, and wailing babies. Parents did what they could to protect the younger children, but all we had to cover ourselves with were the bug-infested life jackets stored at the back of the "shelves." Our baggage, as such, was still on deck. Toward evening, we were allowed up on deck for some tea. We were then allowed to use the "sanitary" facilities.

Once back in the hold, a group of people began to sing Christmas carols. I remember that this was the first time I had heard the carol, "Angels, We Have Heard on High." A group of Roman Catholic sisters in the compartment next to us had started the singing. It was hard to think of angels in high places when, in reality, we were below the ocean's surface, totally shut out of the heavens and at the mercy of our captors.

Surely this is a dream, I thought. I will wake up tomorrow and find it to be the Christmas Day I had always known. All the houses would be festooned with paper lanterns, and there would be presents at the bottom of our palm Christmas tree. The scratching of a rat across my leg shattered that dream in a split second.

We grew braver with the singing, and soon everyone was joining in. All of a sudden we heard:

"Shut up you white monkeys. The captain cannot sleep."

A few of the Japanese sailors and soldiers had crept down

the companionway to listen to the singing and were obviously enjoying the music when this order pierced the air. They left post haste, hoping to escape detection from the higher ups.

Silence prevailed. We had learned by now to accept orders without visible evidence of resentment. Only the sound of crying babies and squealing varmints broke the silence. The ship rocked gently at anchor. Everywhere in the hold was life, and everywhere life was restless and hot.

Morning was ushered in by the clattering of cranes filling up the center of the hold with more army supplies. We heard shuffling about the decks with much yelling and grunting.

Our internee interpreter ventured up the stairway to ask about provisions for feeding us. Our captors had commandeered the food we had brought from the kitchen at Davao. We had not eaten anything for almost twenty-four hours.

"Oh yes, the Imperial Japanese Command take care of all matters. You hully on deck now!" came the reply.

We scrambled up the stairway, all the while trying to adjust to the bright sunlight. Our arrival on deck was just in time to see the last strands of our Christmas dinner of seaweed being hauled up over the side of the ship. We were told that there was no fresh water for drinking for the adults, but there was plenty of hot tea. It tasted as if it were made with seawater. Accompanying the seaweed was a scoop of rice. Worms and bugs were visible. We took our first nourishment without comment.

What was hard to swallow, though, was the sight of the soldiers squatting on the deck helping themselves to the contents of American Red Cross comfort kits. As we choked down the seaweed, we observed them helping themselves to cans of peaches and corned beef.

The soldiers and sailors aboard ship were clad, or unclad depending on how you looked at it, in G-strings. Some were stark naked as they roamed the ship scrutinizing their strange human cargo.

How did we wash ourselves or our eating utensils? Well, some scooped hot tea out of the vat and rinsed the dishes that way. Mother would not let us touch the "fresh" water offered to the children. After a couple of days, the Japanese were asked about our being able to take "showers." We were told that we could use the salt-water hoses up on the deck. The soldiers and sailors all squatted around on the hatch prepared for a show. Well, the men and boys did remove their shirts while the women and girls hosed off fully dressed. So solly to disappoint.

What of the "bathroom" facilities? At the railing on one side of the ship, there were two sorts of kennels, one for men, the other for women. At the back of the "kennel" ran the scupper, which took the water from the deck and directed it to the ocean. From time to time, the men had to take the hoses filled with seawater and hose down these foul troughs.

Save for meals and using the latrines, we remained in the sticky hold. We were constantly worried about being torpedoed. Our ship bore no sign that war prisoners (and civilians at that) were being transported. A huge gash in the side of the vessel told us that the ship had already been attacked.

After three days the ship stopped at the port of Zamboanga, home to many of us on board. We stood at the deck's railing watching Filipinos who paddled out to the ship in little boats. Former students, occupants of one of the boats, recognized us and offered up some soap and am pao be. "Mattocks not pay for this, they shouted!" The Japanese pointed their guns at the visitors and dispersed the flotilla of bancas. We were ordered not to make any contact and were hustled below. My father was up on deck later that night to use the facilities when one of the soldiers came up to him and told him that the waters were alive with American submarines. Daddy made no sort of comment on this but hoped that the Filipinos who had paddled out to the ship might have made some contact with the resistance forces to report the prisoners aboard.

We sailed on toward Manila. The ship was coaled in Cebu. By then, it was New Year's Eve. There was revelry amongst all the crew and soldiers. The sake and tuba were flowing freely. From down below, we could hear loud singing and general merrymaking topside. We could have sung carols all night long for all anyone cared. Suddenly there was a loud thunk, and the boat seemed to just stop from what we could tell. Well, the captain in a drunken stupor had run aground on a sandbar. Toward morning, at high tide, the boat lifted off, and we were on our way.

One morning upon waking, we noticed through the gloom

that the elderly man in the compartment across from us had failed to make any move. It didn't take long to discover that poor Mr. Clemens had died during the night. We watched as his body was covered, removed and taken on deck. The Japanese allowed my father to conduct a brief service as his body was "buried" at sea. The ship plowed on and did not make the customary stop in the ocean to honor the departed. Mr. Clemens was committed to the deep with as dignified manner as could be mustered up under the circumstances.

On January 2, 1944 we steamed into Manila Bay and tied up at Pier 7- the very same pier that before the war had been the scene of gala bon voyage and welcoming parties, complete with streamers and bands. With no bands of welcoming at this docking, we disembarked, boarded army trucks, and found ourselves taken through the streets of Manila to Santo Tomas Internment Camp.

(1) Frank Cary, *Letters from Internment, Davao and Manila, 1942-1945* (Ashland Oregon: Independent Printing Company, 1993), p. 37.

9 / SANTO TOMAS

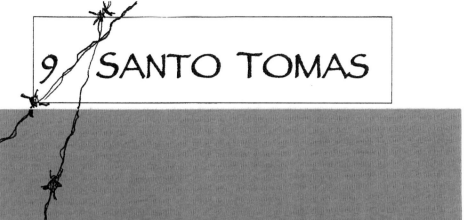

A.V.H. Hartendorp, an official historian of Santo Tomas, writes in his book, *The Santo Tomas Story*:

> Santo Tomas had a number of times been alarmed by the rumor that the internees from Davao, so long expected, had been lost at sea on their way to Manila, but on Sunday, the second day of 1944 came the report that they had at last arrived in Manila and would be brought into camp that day. Not until dusk that evening did the first contingent arrive, a large group of dirty, tired, starved-looking men, women, and children crowded into five buses and army trucks which one after the other drove into a roped off space in front of the Commandant's office. All of Santo Tomas was there to see them come in, but no greetings were permitted until the new arrivals had been registered-an exasperatingly slow process.

He goes on to say:

> It was nine o'clock before all of the 279 internees from Davao and their baggage were in the camp. Ravenously eating the crude Santo Tomas supper, "peanut loaf" and drinking thin tea, they told of their trip. (1)

We joined a camp population of about four thousand Americans, British, and other Allied nationals. The children under eighteen numbered close to eight hundred. Santo Tomas University, founded in 1611, was run by the Dominican order of priests. The imposing Main Building stood at the center of the campus. To the left was the Seminary building (not part of the prison camp), which housed the priests of the order, many of whom were Spaniards and not interned. To the right was the fairly modern looking Education Building that men and boys occupied. At the rear were several outbuildings including an annex, where mothers with babies stayed. In front of the Seminary building was the Gymnasium building occupied by men, many of whom were Spanish-American war veterans. The campus encompassed an area of sixty acres.

Our straggling group was amazed at the fairly good condition of the quarters as well as the comparatively healthy look of the inmates. These internees had been behind the walls for two years already. Why the difference? Many of the interned were from the city of Manila or close by. After the initial herding of enemy civilian nationals into the university grounds, the Japanese began to allow connections on the "outside" to bring articles of clothing, bedding, cooking utensils as well as some small household furnishings and books to their friends on the "inside. " In addition to having a few "luxuries" of their former lives brought in from the outside, some people were recipients of food and other items. At the main gate, under the watchful eyes of the guards, these offerings were received at what was known as the "package line." It should be noted, however, that many internees did not have access to the extras. Some imprisoned just happened to be in Manila on December 8 and were caught there. Others did not have the network of outside friends from the Filipino community. The Japanese at that point however, could afford to be magnanimous. After all, they had conquered most of Southeast Asia in record time.

The Mindanao group was heartened by the appearance of the Manila camp as well as the relative well-being of the interned. We had just experienced ten days of hell in the hold of the *Shinsei Maru*. We had eaten hoofs and heads and were now being served "peanut loaf"!

We were to discover in a short time, however, that the stint at Happy Life Blues had prepared us somewhat for the days of deprivation and starvation, which were soon to come.

From a friend's mother's diary:

> On the second of January, the people from the Davao camp arrived. They were glad to be with us and have their long trip behind them....We had been expecting the arrival of these people for days. They looked strong enough but they were terribly dirty from the trip and the trip on that dirty Japanese ship was a nightmare These people had been

further from supplies of shoes and clothing and their stock of these things was pitifully low.

Many years later, a good friend wrote about the 1944 Davao arrivals. Unfortunately, she had just "lost" her braids due to a common infestation. She recalls meeting me in a scene she describes in a piece entitled, "Braids of Friendship," which she wrote for one of the camp reunions.

Excerpted from that piece:

> Then one evening into camp came the prisoners from Davao. The troop trucks crowded with standing people lurched to a stop at the main plaza of Santo Tomas. Watching from our Main Building room window, I glimpsed a small figure whose long, blond braids shone through the dusky tropical twilight. Drawn as if by a magnetic force, I rushed down to my assigned task of welcoming the arriving children. And there she was, an alter ego...my age, my size, my hair! Those braids entwined me at once in friendship. And with a new friend, I could become a new me.

> Fifty years later, after being apart, we rediscovered each other at the Las Vegas prison camp reunion-though we are both without braids, our bond of friendship remains just as strong.

Mother, Shirley, and I were assigned to room 30A on the second floor of the Main Building, a former dean's office. Fifty women and girls shared these quarters. We were issued a slatted wooden cot each and bare bones mattresses. The allotted space measured about four by seven feet, per person. We were accustomed to crowded sleeping quarters. We shoved the three cots together to make more aisle space in which to navigate; this enabled us to be a few inches further from the next sleepers. Other than a set of bamboo shelves, there was no other furniture. We kept everything under the beds. Fortunately, our set of cots abutted a window which, at times, gave us a bit of a breeze and later, a ringside seat to watch the bombings.

My father and brother were on the third floor, room 54, in the same building. Their space ration was similar. Boys under six years of age were allowed to be with their mothers.

The bathroom for the floor was at the end of the hallway right outside the door to our room. Five showerheads lined one side of the room and five toilets lined the other. There were no doors on the stalls. Privacy was nonexistent: a luxury not experienced since the beginning of the war. One of the camp duties was the meting out of toilet paper. A woman, in our case, stood outside the door and issued one or two squares of paper to each person waiting in the long line. Having inside facilities was certainly an improvement over the "benjo" trek in Davao.

In the Main Building there were eleven toilets for 750 women. (2)

Meal tickets were issued to each of us. We ate, at first, in the dining sheds at the back of the Main Building next to the kitchens. The latter were open-air structures under tin roofs. The food was cooked using gas, and augmented by firewood when the gas gave out. Most of it was cooked in huge cawas. These great pots had to be carried into the serving area, which was at the back entrance of the building. We spent many hours standing in the chow line. We carried pails made of old tin cans with wire handles. Most of the food was sloppy. If we did get rice, we used a separate tin or a coconut shell. We didn't want to be the next person in line to be served when a fresh pot was brought in. We knew that the few beans and bits of meat, if there were any, had sunk to the bottom. Sometimes we children let a few people get in front of us so that we would have the goodies closer to the bottom.

Shortly after our arrival, each member of the Davao group was issued one Red Cross comfort kit. The other internees had received theirs earlier. There had been many shipments of these kits during the war from the various Red Cross organizations. This particular distribution was the only one we ever received. The kits, about fifty pounds each, contained among other items, Spam, corned beef, bouillon cubes, canned salmon, powdered milk (KLIM), butter (tinned), a few packets of sugar, chocolate, tooth powder, cigarettes, and small bars of soap. The soap wrappers were printed with the acronym, GAYLA. We thought it meant "Greetings All You Loyal Americans!" Some people dove right into their kits and feasted for a few days. Mother insisted that we save ours for a time when she was sure these extras would save our lives. We stowed the kits under the beds and guarded them fiercely.

Strangely, some people craved nicotine so badly that even though they were starving, they were willing to trade cans of corned beef and other food commodities from their kits for cigarettes. In addition, some of the kids in the camp scooped up the discarded cigarette butts from the soldiers. These they used to barter for a piece of chocolate, a piece of sugar cane, or whatever the smoker was willing to part with for a butt.

In addition to the food, there was a shipment of "play suits" for the women. Soon many women were wearing pink, blue, or green variations of the same style. There were some shoes distributed, but in my diary I reported that none fit me. Most of the girls were comfortable in their bakyas anyway.

A well-organized school had been established and had functioned since the early days of STIC. There were classes from kindergarten through college. The classes we attended were held in the open air laboratories and classrooms on the fourth floor of the Main Building.

Among the internees were many teachers and college professors. Supplies of paper, notebooks, and pencils were limited, and, at times, nonexistent. We all shared textbooks. At my level, English, mathematics, and history were taught during morning classes. In the beginning of the camp while people still had the energy to conduct or partake of classes, there were offerings of languages, philosophy, literature, music, etc., for adults by those knowledgeable in those fields. Shortly after our arrival, the extra offerings were discontinued as the conditions in the camp had declined.

Before our arrival at Santo Tomas, there had been some fairly sophisticated shows put on by the dramatically and musically-talented internees. But by the time we got there, these performances were pretty much a thing of the past. The Japanese did show propaganda films occasionally on the large outdoor screen. I don't know how many times we saw the American navy being sunk. I became aware at these movies that my eyesight was deteriorating and the great sea battles being shown were all a blur to me. As in Davao, choral groups were formed. Before dusk on some evenings a variety of music would be played on the public address system. But, like the other entertainment, all this came to a halt when the focus of the entire camp was on the lack of food.

As in Davao, the camp had a democratic structure organized by the internees. Leaders were elected to do specific jobs and for specific terms. From the Chairman of the camp to the Chairman of Sanitation, every duty was spelled out. Since Mother was a teacher, she was assigned to teach grade four. My father's first assignment was policing the ladies peeling the vegetables. This proved to be embarrassing at times, as he had to speak to prominent members of the community about stuffing camote peelings down the fronts of their blouses. Careful attention was paid to the thickness of the peelings.

During the last few months of internment, there weren't too many vegetables to peel; the peeling crew was disbanded and the few vegetables that were available were added to the stew, peels and all. My father's second assignment was gatekeeper at the main gate. He had to open and close the gates for the arrival and departure of the Japanese officials. When the bombings started, this proved to be a busy and risky job because many of the high mucky mucks in the city would seek refuge in the relative safety of Santo Tomas. At the same time, it was dangerous during the bombings, because besides the fear of being hit by falling shrapnel, one was tempted to look up at the bombers and the dog fights that invariably ensued. To do so one would incur the punishment of standing in the hot sun looking skyward. He was also a room monitor. Aside from trying to keep peace among the sometimes-fractious group in the room, he was responsible for order and proper bowing at roll call.

As a twelve-year old, I with others my age, was required to do garden work. The detail would be called to the front plaza. A bayoneted guard would escort the group to the garden area under cultivation. We weeded, sweltering in the blistering sun, under the watchful eye of the soldier. However, we were never able to reap any of the rewards of this labor, because as soon as the plants were ripe for picking, the area was declared out of bounds.

A month after our arrival, the Japanese military took over the running of the camp. With the military takeover, many of the advantages some of the internees had, like the package line, were discontinued. They also took over much of the buying of food. They ordered everyone who had pesos to turn the currency in to be deposited in the Bank of Taiwan. It was forbidden to have more than a few pesos in one's possession.

Roll call was ordered. Twice a day we stood to be counted; we were counted in the morning before breakfast and in the evening after supper. We stood by twos for as few as thirty minutes: yet at times the ritual lasted two hours.

It was the room monitor's job to keep everyone in order until the Japanese officer passed by. It was also her responsibility to see that everyone bowed properly from the waist, and in unison. Bowing practice was conducted regularly. It was difficult keeping fidgety children at attention. We stood somewhat informally until we heard the counting officer coming down the corridor, announced by the clumping of his heavily booted foot and his long saber clanking against it. Sometimes we were routed out of bed to be counted in the middle of the night. At other times an announcement would come over the loudspeaker that a roll call was to be held immediately.

Of all the restrictions we had placed on us, none was as irritating as roll call and the order to bow.

From the Commandant:

All internees, men women and children shall bow to Japanese officers, soldiers, clerks and to all Japanese attached to the Japanese administration of this camp and also to Japanese visitors in uniform. Bowing should be from the waist. When bowed to in the proper manner, the Japanese officers will acknowledge with a salute or a bow.(3)

The guards had frequent inspections, sometimes announced and sometimes at whim. These inspections could be conducted any time of day or night. Sometimes certain rooms were targeted. More often the whole camp was turned upside down. They were always looking for radio equipment, writings of various sorts, or money that was illegal to hold. News from the outside was creeping into camp, and the Japanese were at their wits' ends trying to find the source. Later, I learned, that rudimentary receiving sets were assembled in secret spots and disassembled as soon as a broadcast was heard. The parts were hidden separately in various hiding places. To have been discovered in this venture would have meant certain death to those conducting this operation. Most of us got the "news" via the loudspeaker system. The broadcaster was a well-known Manila radio announcer and was able to slip in various tidbits of information amongst the usual calls for details or summons to the Commandant's office. For example, when the news of the Americans landing on the island of Leyte reached those with a radio connection, he ended his broadcast with, "Better Leyte than never!" One time, when there were rumors of the arrival of Red Cross comfort kits, he played the piece, "Pennies from Heaven!" "Ding, Dong the Witch is Dead" was played when there were rumors of Hitler's death. Communications of all sorts-from the air raid warnings to the ever-changing rules-were transmitted by the public address system.

The following two ditties are examples of attempts to make the mundane interesting:

> Good morning folks
> At the sound of the chime
> Twill be just 6:30
> STIC standard time.

> We're giving a call
> To the fish cleaning crew
> Come one, come all
> And help make the fish stew.

There was a jail within the camp. For infractions of the internee rules, punishment was meted out by a committee assigned to that task. Pilfering, altercations that went beyond words, and misdemeanors could get one a sentence and confinement to the jail. It was better to keep the lawbreakers out of the eyes of the Japanese guards whose punishment would be far worse. However, occasionally internees were whisked out of camp for what, at the moment, appeared to be no apparent reason. Usually, the destination was Fort Santiago, an imposing fortress built during the days of the Spanish occupation. Torture and punishment at the fort were brutal. It would surface later that perhaps the accused were under suspicion of having communicated with the outside or "over the wall. " Perhaps they were involved with those in the resistance movement. In any case, if they were returned to camp, they did not reveal the brutalities at Fort Santiago until after the war.

Within Santo Tomas, most punishment by the guards was restricted to slappings. Slappings across the face were the quick punishment of choice among the hierarchy of the guards also. A few times, I was to witness the screaming of those being beaten or otherwise tortured outside the walls of the camp. Sympathetic Filipinos communicated with some of the inmates by timing the guard's beat and then at a "safe" period sending messages or packages over the wall. When caught, the punishment was severe for both the sender and the receiver.

From *Father John Mears, Ninety Years,* (Father Mears, one of our mission priests published this book on the occasion of his ninetieth birthday):

None of us was beaten at any time by Japanese guards, though we could not doubt their intentions to break our spirit. However, we did see examples of tortured bodies that came in under the seal of secrecy not to divulge what they had seen in the former Spanish Fort Santiago. The people were quiet and wooden faced. One wondered if they would or could ever again talk freely without the fear of being seized and subjected to torture. (4)

Because of the overcrowding in the Main Building, many of the internees who had the wherewithal to do so were allowed to build nipa shanties in the outer areas of the campus. For the most part, these were shelters for daylight hours, places to eat, and to have a little privacy. These shanty areas were given names like: Froggy Bottom, Shantytown, and Glamourville among others. There were periods when overnight stays were allowed. In addition, another camp was opened in Los Banos, south of Manila. Many volunteered to be sent there. The camp was erected on the site of an agricultural college.

Those who chose to go felt that they would be able to better supplement their diet by planting more of their own food. Several of our mountain friends made the choice to be transferred to Los Banos. It was hard saying goodbye to them. After all, we had been together since the first days of the war.

In the east patio of the Main Building, some people had built cook shanties. These were rude structures of a lean-to type.

Because of the Los Banos exodus, one of these became available and my parents were able to secure it. The roof was constructed of nipa and two sides were of sawali (woven bamboo). The other sides were open. It was furnished with a bamboo table and two benches. A rudimentary stove was made out of an old kerosene tin. It was here that our family now met to eat, rather than in the eating sheds or in the upstairs hallway where there were a few tables and chairs. It was the only time we were together during the day. As children, we were left fairly free to roam or congregate with friends when we were not having classes or on a detail.

Mother spent hours hunched over a miserable few pieces of charcoal or wood trying to coax a bit of heat from the fire. She grew a few sprigs of talinum or what we called "slippery greens" beside the hut. She'd add a few of these leaves or other greens to the food from the chow line.

From my diary:

> Bob W. came by and gave us some gabi (taro) leaves to cook.

Our utensils were few. For the collection of food from the line, we used the tin cans I mentioned. We had saved some of our coconut shell dishes from the mountains, and we had a few pieces of silverware. At one point, we were allowed to take our rice ration raw. Mother opted for this because she felt she could cook it and clean it better than the kitchen crew did. After a while toward the end, no one cared if was cleaned or not, although we did try to pick out the worms that were floating on top.

There were two or three areas where the sick were confined. Santa Catalina Hospital was the facility, which had the most beds. It was situated outside the wall on the east side of the campus. There were several doctors, among the interned, as well as two or three who were transferred from the military prisoner-of-war camps. There were several civilian nurses as well as a large contingent of military nurses that was brought into Santo Tomas after the fall of Corregidor. Many of these nurses felt their places were with the military and not with civilians. However, they performed their duties admirably, and the camp would have been hard pressed to provide the services they contributed.

Medicine was difficult to obtain. I learned years later that there was a well-organized underground network for the procurement of medical supplies as well as some food supplies. At the time, I was not aware of all the intrigue and wheelings and dealings that went on for our benefit. Since privacy was at a premium, sometimes we children were privy to all sorts of whisperings and conversations that gave us information to process that would have been far beyond our years had the times been normal.

Courageous and sympathetic Filipinos with the help of a few of the uninterned padres in the adjacent Seminary Building conducted a secret smuggling system right under the noses of the captors. These people left themselves open to torture and execution had they been discovered. Without this supplemental assistance there would have much more untreated sickness and certainly more deaths.

I spent a few weeks in Santa Catalina Hospital, as I was plagued with a series of ear infections and fevers of undetermined origin. The ward I was assigned to had about thirty beds. Privacy did not exist. The aged and those twelve and above were side by side. As I think back on it, I don't know how anyone got better. One was awake all night with the moaning of those about to die and patients, like myself, who almost "enjoyed" being there because the food was "one up" on the chow line. I was surprised how quickly death came. Someone would be crying out, and in the next moment there would be silence. Death. The fine line between life and death amazed and even frightened me.

Early on in our internment at STIC, I had a tonsillectomy performed in an effort to stave off the constant fevers and infections. Although there were the usual bouts of measles, chicken pox, and dengue fever, there were no mass outbreaks of dreaded diseases that one would associate with living in such close quarters with less than optimum sanitation conditions.

The sanitation committee did its best. Even so, bedbugs were rampant. They would bury themselves in the corners of the mosquito netting and the mattresses. A daily chore was to squash as many of the bugs you could pick out to ward off being bitten during the night.

As the starvation period progressed, many of the diseases associated with vitamin and nutritional deficiencies began to appear. Beriberi was prevalent. People whose rib cages were fairly bare of flesh were being supported by legs that resembled those of elephants. In some cases, the legs were split by the fluid that could no longer be retained under the skin. Both Mother and Daddy suffered from this disease. At this point my father's weight was fifty pounds under his pre-war weight, and Mother weighed only eighty-nine pounds. Normal maturation among the girls was delayed. Women ceased having periods. Many people suffered from tooth decay, eyesight, or hearing problems. Dysentery was widespread and for many, gastric problems continued for many years after we were liberated.

The older children pretty much had free rein to be on their own. We occupied ourselves with school when it was held or played the usual kids' games like cat's cradle. A lady in the camp decided to hold knitting classes for the girls. Somehow she obtained balls and balls of variegated orange and yellow string. She prevailed upon a man to make bamboo knitting needles. She taught us all how to make socks or in some cases, underpants, both of which were very rough on the skin. Another woman had some scraps of fabric, and she had some of us making little teddy bears. Because we were interned on a university campus, we had access to some of the books that were stored in a first floor classroom. In addition, in the early days some people had brought books in from the outside. The library was a cool place to hide out of the heat. I think I read the *Compton's* Encyclopedia from cover to cover. Almost every afternoon found me there poring over reference books or immersing myself in the Elsie Dinsmore series of stories.

One phenomenon experienced by just about everyone was the obsessive copying of recipes. Many of these were given orally, and men and women alike copied them down on any scrap of paper they could scrounge up. We discovered later that this recipe craze was repeated in all the civilian camps as well as the military ones. I never heard of anyone making any of the dishes after the war, but the fantasies of doing so filled many hours of daydreaming about the day when we would be free from hunger. Every night the last words of the lady in the next bed to ours was about gobs of whipped cream.

During the last six months of internment, the food situation deteriorated daily. Although the Japanese did supply a very meager amount of food, much of it was inedible. Sometimes they would send in tons of fish that had rotted long before it had reached the camp. Much of the rice consisted of sweepings off bodega floors. The soybeans were pretty much refuse. Sometimes the evening "stew" which was reduced to a puree by now, would have a few mongo beans floating in it; sometimes shreds of unidentifiable meat made its way into the cawas. We suspected that this was carabao and later pigeon. Later, because the dogs and cats on the campus were disappearing, we had a feeling that they ended up in the communal pot also. We didn't ask.

Sometimes at lunch a smelly fish paste was served, and at times little fishes called "dilis" were dished out with heads and tails intact. These fish were about two inches long and very salty. Hungry as I was, I couldn't bear to eat the head.

Toward the end of internment, people were seen foraging for scraps of food in the garbage cans of the guards. Occasionally, warnings had to be issued about eating certain plants that grew around the campus, as they were poisonous. Several around our cook shanty tried to cook garden slugs. They were reported to be very rubbery.

Even under these circumstances, humor played a vital role. Each week a clever cartoonist drew a scene from camp life on a blackboard hung on a wall behind the serving line. Always, there was some innuendo about the captors hidden in the drawings. From the book *How We Took It* by Albert J Stahl, the following poem makes light of the disappearing cats and dogs.

FILET DE CHAT

Ding dong bell
Our cat tasted swell
Not too tough and not too sweet,
Very much like chicken meat,
Sure it was a treat.

Ding dong bell
Our pooch looks swell.
The old woman will be vexed
I'm just looking for pretext
And her Fido will be next,
Ding dong bell. (5)

Some entries from my diary give an indication of the effort that was made to augment the line food by whatever means we could:

....Had thin mush for breakfast. Saw many planes. We made a casserole with pechay (like spinach) and talinum (also like spinach). Later when we went down to the cook shack for supper, one fourth of it was gone. Stolen!

....Mush for breakfast was solid. Daddy saved his until lunch. Scavenged for greens.

....Had camote tops (sweet potato leaves) for supper and part of the last bouillon cube.

....Had the rest of the bouillon cube for lunch. Line soup tasted like chicken (I am sure it wasn't).

....Cooked mush. Had sweetened water for breakfast.

....Awfully hungry. I weigh 72 pounds now, (I weighed 72 pounds when the war began). Got skimpy raw rice. Allotted 223 grams of raw rice for three meals.

....Again, watery mush. We took the beans out of the stew and cooked them with the pechay. Escalante!!!

....Changed meal ticket to 14 meals a week basis

Toward August of 1944, conditions in camp were on the decline at a rapid rate. Blackout was instituted so people retired early. We could hear small explosions throughout the city. The guards conducted bayonet drills with accompanying savage yells and grunts. Antiaircraft practice was a daily event. The Japanese brought in, for storage and protection from bombs, all sorts of oil drums, small machines and metal parts. These were stacked up next to the plaza. Some of the younger children were curious and clambered all over the stockpiles. They were warned by the guards to keep away. A few of the beautiful trees, which lined the roadway into the camp, had to be chopped for firewood. A Japanese buyer now did the food buying with money from internees, a meager allowance from the military, and funds from the Red Cross. Food supplies were becoming scarce in the city. The Japanese currency printed locally was known as "Mickey Mouse." There was some back biting in camp as some felt that the children should be rationed smaller allowances of food. Some traded rings, fountain pens, and watches with the guards who were willing to take the risk. A diamond ring bought a kilo of rice or sugar.

An example of prices of commodities on December 31,1944:

Sugar, one kilo	(equivalent of US)	$105.
Evaporated milk 20 oz. can		$ 20.
Rice,one kilo		$ 60.
Vegetable lard, one pound		$ 90.(6)

As people became weaker and the procurement of food took all one's time and strength, there was not much energy left over for amusement. People sat in the corridors or in the shanty areas talking about food or "getting out of here," and not much else. Father John Mears describes the scene for his daughter:

The constant daily care of you, dear Kathleen, was a joy. But, from time to time, a dear little ten year old [I was twelve] neighbor girl, Cecily Mattocks, (daughter of Rev. and Mrs. Henry Mattocks) would come by in the evening and baby sit you for an hour or two. With the stress of our lives and the heavy work, this was a precious gift. To be able to spend time chatting with other parents and friends in the darkened halls of Santo Tomas was a special respite. These times were like precious stones in a necklace-a sweet offering beyond human price. (7)

At one point, the Japanese demanded that everyone sign an oath of allegiance. At first, many refused or signed with an "under protest" notation under their signature. In the end, all except one signed, the holdout being a Chinese-American who, in addition to not signing, had pledged to wear the same shirt until we were liberated. At liberation, there was one shred of fabric draped across his shoulder. His punishment for not signing was confinement to the camp jail. The oath:

I, the undersigned, hereby solemnly pledge myself that I will not under any circumstances attempt to escape or conspire directly or indirectly against the Japanese Military Authorities as long as I am in their custody. (8)

Next to the day of our liberation, September 21, 1944 was a glorious one. We children were up on the fourth floor having our classes. There had been some antiaircraft practice earlier in the morning. We heard the drone of planes, but then, Japanese planes flew over regularly. Yet suddenly, as the detonation of bombs shook the earth, we bolted from our seats, ran out, and looked into the sky that was filled with what seemed to be hundreds of silver planes. Wave upon wave of American bombers were flying in perfect formation above the range of the white puffs of the antiaircraft fire. They delivered their deadly payload, and then another group came over and repeated the performance. Clearly, the Japanese had been totally surprised. Soon there were fires all over the bombed areas. Belatedly, the air raid siren sounded.

Excitement and emotions ran high. Surely, the army must be close behind. Some even dove into the remnants of their comfort kits and had a feast. Not so, Mother. For her, the worst hadn't come yet.

From *The Santo Tomas Story,* Hartendorp quotes from Admiral Halsey:

We hit them four times on the 21st and expected to hit them four times the next day, but the approach of foul weather and the dearth of suitable targets influenced me to cancel the last two strikes. His (Vice-Admiral Marc A. Mitscher) score for the six was 405 planes destroyed or damaged, 103 ships sunk or damaged, both airfields gutted, and the harbor littered with wrecks. Our losses were 15 planes and about a dozen men. None of our ships was touched although we had launched from only 40 miles off the east coast of Luzon less than 150 miles from Manila itself. (9)

Years later, at a speaking engagement in Worcester, Massachusetts, I met two men who told me they had been pilots who had participated in that and other air strikes over Manila.

They were quite emotional, even fifty-five years later. Until that point, they had remembered being concerned with their bombing targets and not with the fact that thousands of feet below were many of their countrymen confined in prisons, cheering every blast and explosion that would bring their deliverance one day closer.

After the initial discombobulation of the guards following the surprise attack, they settled down to issuing some rules:

1. Absolutely no looking up at the planes or dog fights.

2. Guards will be posted below windows to enforce this.

3. Punishment, if caught, was to be taken to the guard house and forced to stand for hours looking at the sun.

Many thought that after the September 21st bombing, release would occur in a matter of days. Many days of constant bombing followed the initial raid, followed by days of no action. Sometimes there were great displays of divebombing. There was an airfield off the northeast corner of the Main Building at Grace Field. Since we were forbidden to look out the window, Shirley, and I would lie on our cots and watch the planes hurtle nose down, one by one, drop their bombs, and be up and away before the antiaircraft guns were activated. During the bombings, I personally saw only one American plane go down, although there were several, which met this fate. The plane, after being hit with antiaircraft fire, exploded in the air; and in a few seconds several of the airmen were seen floating down over the city, their parachutes unfurled above them, and their fate sealed in the hands of the waiting enemy below.

Strange to say, we looked forward to the bombings, though they came with a price. We were disappointed when days went by, and no siren wailed its eerie warning.

It was to be almost five months before the longed-for freedom was to become a reality. At Christmastime 1944, energy and morale were low. The deaths were increasing. Starvation stalked the camp. Just before Christmas, leaflets were dropped from planes flying over the camp.They read:

The Commander-in-Chief, the officers and men of the American forces of Liberation of the Pacific, wish their gallant allies, the people of the Philippines, all the blessings of Christmas and the realization of their fervent hopes for the New Year. Christmas 1944. (10)

There was severe punishment for having one of these leaflets in one's possession.

Our fourth Christmas of war was at hand. Presents were limited to drawings done on scraps of paper, poems copied and put together in a notebook sewn together with thread. We sang the familiar carols as we had before and hoped, as we had before, that the next Christmas would find us free.

Louise Goldthorpe, the mission nurse at Brent Hospital in Zamboanga, was a great friend of Mother's. Many years after the war, she sent excerpts of her wartime diary to our family as enclosures in her Christmas cards.

From Louise Goldthorpe's diary:

December 25, 1944 American planes fly over and drop leaflets. ...Later we went over to watch the children having a party. Each child was given a piece of coconut candy made with brown sugar. There was great rejoicing over this treat.

Mother tried to keep our spirits up. The occupants of Room 30A were a mixed lot who were becoming ill-tempered, restless, and dispirited. In addition to the hunger, the bombings, the daily addition of restrictions, and the general lassitude, many were losing hope that freedom would ever come. The imposed curfew sent people into the building earlier. In addition, "all clears" were not sounded even though the raids for which they had been activated were over. Restrictions for air raids, therefore, were in place for hours, even days. Those who rationed their comfort kits against the time of starvation were envied by those whose kits had long been devoured. We were glad to be eating in the cook shanty where the little extras Mother was able to scrounge up would not be observed by others. Thoughts of food, or the lack of it, controlled every waking moment.

Several years ago, I went to visit a woman in Arizona who, with her two young children, had slept across the aisle on one side of us. She told me that Mother was the glue who kept the room together. When there were outbreaks of frustration and despair, she encouraged those who became mired in hopelessness and negativism to carry on, and to have faith that we would be rescued.

I do not have any letter as I did in Davao to tell me what she was really feeling. Yet, on the surface, she never resorted to pessimism. Always, she started her sentences with, "When we get out of here." She made us believe that that day would come.

(1) A.V.H. Hartendorp, *The Santo Tomas Story* (New York: McGraw Hill Book Company, 1964) pp. 209-210.
(2) Ibid, p. 216.
(3) Ibid, p. 341.
(4) John Mears, *John Mears, Ninety Years* (Privately Published), 2002, p. 105.
(5) Albert J. Stahl, *How We Took It* (New York: Privately Published), 1945, p. 50.
(6) *Liberation Bulletin of Philippine Internment Camp at Santo Tomas University* (Norfolk, Virginia: Courtesy of MacArthur Museum Archives).
(7) John Mears, p. 99.
(8) A.V.H. Hartendorp, p. 254.
(9) Ibid, p. 322 from Admiral Halsey's Story, McGraw Hill, 1947.
(10) A.V.H. Hartendorp, p. 372.

10 LAST DAYS

The Japanese continued conducting the demolition of ammunition dumps, reserves of oil, and other supplies that might be useful to the returning United States troops. The days were punctuated by explosions with the resulting raging fires. Added to this were the continued bombing raids by American planes, and the explosions of antiaircraft fire. Thankfully, these missiles missed their mark most of the time. The night sky was alive with bands of searchlights crisscrossing in a sweep of the heavens. I remember the roosters crowing all night long because the light from the fires had fooled them into thinking it was early morning.

Not only were the crackling fires licking the walls of the camp, but we could feel the scorching heat from them as well. The woman in the next bed to ours kept up an anguished cry that we were all going to burn to death. For a while, I thought she was right.

There was gunfire both distant and close by. Restlessness stalked the guards as well as the internees. The guards in the Education Building next to the Main Building were seen burning their documents and papers. There was no escape from the inferno that raged beyond the walls. The tremendous detonations, which shook the building night and day, were unnerving. Sleep was difficult.

Despite this, although fraught with lethargy and apathy, prison life went on, even as the area was being swallowed up in flames and deafening explosions rattled people's nerves. By now, people were so weak that they simply spent their days sitting around talking about whether the troops would get to Manila in time to save us. In the last stages of starvation, some internees could barely muster up enough energy to stand for the required roll calls or shuffle off to the chow lines.

Meals, by this time, were restricted to two a day. Some people, including our family, had nursed their comfort kits along so that there might be a couple of cans of corned beef or Spam left with which to augment or flavor the mush. Entries from my diary at this period indicate that daily living centered around the all-important mush or lugao, we saved from the chow line and any sort of "extra" we could add to it:

....I cooked mush. Mother in bed. Copied recipes. Geoffrey got rice crisp from the bottom of the cawa. (scrapings that sometimes were handed out to the children when the pots were being cleaned).

....I cooked mush. Saw three U.S. planes as low as house tops. Huge explosions and fires continue. Daddy is on raw rice again (so we can cook our own). Terribly hungry.

....Cooked mush. Wash mosquito nets (filled with bed bugs). Lots of demolition and fires. Cooked spinach stalks. Got hard tack on the line. Saved mine for supper. Terrible rain.

....Awful simultaneous bombing. Air raid all night long. Mush for breakfast was solid.

....Air raid continues. Artillery fire all morning. Any minute now!

....Very watery mush. Saw 52 P48's flying very high. Aired mattresses. Full of bedbugs.

....Huge explosions. Lots of demolition and fires. Terribly hungry.

....Air raid at 9:30 p.m. Terrific bombs. Peeled some camotes.

From a friend's diary:

While we were cooking, Mrs. Mattocks said that some woman in the patio was about to throw some sour mush away...Could we use it? So I went over and got it.

Made "pan bread." First time in weeks we got up from supper and felt satisfied.

If there were an air raid in the early morning, then breakfast was a piece of hardtack instead of the customary lugao.

The Kempeitai increased its searches. They arrested Carroll Grinnell, (our elected camp chairman), Mr. Duggleby, Mr. Johnson, and Mr. Larsen. No reasons were given and many pleas for their release were denied. Later, after liberation, their bodies were discovered. They had all been beheaded.

School classes had long since been cancelled. We were all too weak to climb the stairs. The shrapnel from the daily raids made it dangerous to be out in the open on the fourth floor. No "all clear" had been sounded for an air raid that had begun a couple of weeks before. Sometimes the sound of shrapnel falling on the tin roof of the eating sheds sounded like heavy rain. Few Japanese planes intercepted the American bombers now. Blackout and early curfew kept us confined.

Excerpts from Louise Goldthorpe's diary, which she sent to us, graphically describe the last days:

December 23, 1944, I am losing about a pound a day. Fr. Ewing brought me a piece of liver, I asked him what sort of liver it was. He said, "Never mind, just cook it and eat it." Then I knew it was cat. I said, "I can't eat it, but I will cook it for you." From now on, only two meals will be served: Mush at 8 a.m. and mush at 4 p.m.....

December 31, 1944, The Japanese are celebrating in high fashion. New Years is a very special time for them. They are frying meat, roasting peanuts, baking bread. Creating enough good smells to tempt hungry people to commit almost any crime. Reading about food is not as painful as smelling it when you can't have it.

January 15, 1944, Food is getting much shorter. I have a heavy feeling in my chest. It is very hard to find a comfortable position to sleep at night. No water pressure above the first floor. Everyone is trying to cook something over a smoking fire....the trunk of a tree, flower bulbs, all sorts of weeds. There is not a pigeon in the place.

The all-consuming business of trying to keep alive went on, but death also claimed its victims. The hearse that came into the camp originally had now been replaced by a cart drawn by a man whose duty it was to escort the dead from the compound. The sound of the wooden wheels of the cart carrying the deceased was a grim reminder that death was not too far away from many of us. We were helpless to do anything about our situation except pray.

Listing "starvation" as a cause of death on several death certificates angered the Japanese authorities. As a result of his refusal to accede to their demands to change the wording, one of the doctors in the camp resigned, and chose a jail sentence rather than compromise the truth.

From *Father John Mears, Ninety Years:*

During the months of December and January 1944, the death toll mounted. Sometimes we had four or five leave by a side gate in a plain box in a rickety carriage. They were unaccompanied by friends or relatives who would otherwise give parting dignity to the tired wasted body of another human being who had so recently talked and dreamed of freedom and homecoming. (1)

(1) John Mears, *Father John Mears, Ninety Years* (Privately Published), p. 124.

11 LIBERATION

During the late afternoon of February third, several Navy planes flew low over the camp. One of the pilots dropped a pair of flyer's goggles into one of the patios of the Main Building. Contained in the goggles was the message:

Roll out the barrel, Christmas is coming. We'll be with you Sunday or Monday!

There are several variations of these words, but this was Saturday evening, and the important message was that freedom was at hand. It didn't take long for this news to spread through the camp. At roll call time, the room monitors had a struggle trying to get their charges in line for the Japanese inspection. We all stood in ragged formation; the guards clomped through, but they didn't pay much attention. I suspect that at that point, they knew the die was cast in our favor.

We tried to go about our routine. We stood in the chow line amidst much agitation and conjecture about the significance of the dropped message. There wasn't much time after the evening lugao for anything else. There was curfew and blackout, but the darkened halls were far from quiet. An undercurrent of hushed voices filled the corridors. Internees gathered in clusters outside the rooms debating the significance of the "goggle" message and whether Sunday or Monday would be too late.

Before long, though, we began to hear distant rumbling. The building shook. Tracer bullets with their brilliant colors whizzed by the windows. Machine gun fire rattled outside the walls. Mothers frantically tried to keep the children away from the windows. The rumble and drone of distant machinery came closer.

"What were the Japanese doing?" we asked.

We had not heard that particular rumbling noise before. We had long heard rumors of orders for our impending massacre. Many people had claimed to have seen a notice relating to the extermination of prisoners. Was this it? Although nine o'clock was approaching, there was restlessness everywhere. By now the thundering and shaking seemed to be out in the adjacent streets. There were shouts from Filipinos over the wall. Abruptly, the shaking and reverberations stopped.

Suddenly, the air was punctuated with the cries of internees screaming down the hallways: "The Americans are here, the Americans are here!"

My diary entry from that date follows:

February 3   Lots of strafing and bombing. Nine planes flew over camp low. Saw insignia. Heard and saw rockets. A Japanese guard came into the room and shut the windows. Something is up. Total blackout. At nine o'clock American tanks, trucks and troops rolled in the gate! I couldn't go to sleep. I was awake all night.

The euphoric feeling and the exuberance all of us experienced the night of our deliverance on February 3, 1945 is impossible to put into words. In my diary, I simply added:

THE HAPPIEST NIGHT OF OUR LIFES!

From *John Mears, Ninety Years:*

The night will long be remembered as a swirl of faces all lit up with rapturous, unbelieving joy. We were moving by means of a high-powered intoxicant. This was the day, the night of our first taste of freedom from the ever-present Nippon conqueror. If ever Americans felt a kinship for one another, we did that night. These were our brothers returned to save us: huge, brawny men, flesh of our flesh and bone of our bone. (1)

Several hundred men of the Flying Column of the First Cavalry Division supported by the tanks and armored vehicles of the 44th Tank Battalion had raced down to Manila from Lingayan Gulf in the north for the express purpose of liberating Santo Tomas. In the city of Manila, there were thousands of Japanese troops who were taken by surprise with this sudden entrance of American troops.

We were told that word had been received that the Japanese were planning an annihilation of the civilian prisoners within days. General MacArthur's admonition to the First Cavalry's Flying Column and the the 44th Tank Battalion attached to it was:

"Go to Manila. Go around the Nips, bounce off the Nips, but go to Manila! Free the internees at Santo Tomas!...." (2)

The tanks, trucks, armor, and jeeps of the army had been led through the streets of Manila to the gates of Santo Tomas by Captain Manuel Colayco, a Filipino guerilla. Sadly, Colayco was to lose his life in this endeavor. He was downed by a hand grenade thrown by one of the guards at the main gate.

The tanks crashed through the iron gates and lumbered to a stop in the plaza in front of the Main Building. All the while, their searchlights were scanning the buildings. Pandemonium erupted.

There was another shooting. Lt. Abiko, the guard most disliked by the internees, had pulled out a hand grenade as he faced the oncoming tanks. He was shot on the spot. Soldiers carried him to the foyer of the Main Building where he was attended by medics. He died a short time later, but not before some internees expressed their disgust of him.

The internees streamed down the hallways and onto the front plaza. Some people burst into an impromptu "God Bless America." Shirley and I, with others, ran down the back staircase. Mother felt that the front would be too dangerous.... and it was.

Parked at the entrance at the back of the building was the tank "Georgia Peach." Standing next to the tank, dressed in battle garb, were some of the GIs who had just crashed through the gates. I thought they were the tallest men I had ever seen. Years later, at a prison camp reunion attended by some of our liberators, I was surprised to see that they were not the giants I had remembered. To our eyes on that glorious night, they loomed larger than life, as they stood there handing out chocolates and Life Savers.

These men had fought their way up through Guadalcanal, Saipan, New Guinea, and other islands. They were hardened, battle-scarred soldiers. They had not seen American or European women and children for almost three years. Manila was to be their first battleground in a city. Yet, on the night of February third, they were moved by the throngs of emaciated, gaunt, starving countrymen before them.

Outside the wall, there was continued shooting. Tracer bullets were still sizzling through the air. The excitement and thrill of the arrival of our troops made us oblivious to the dangers that surrounded us. We pushed and shoved our way to get a closer look at the men who had staged this daring raid after a three-day race through enemy lines. The lead tank, first to crash through the gates, was called "Battlin' Basic."

Fifty-five years later, the head gunner on this tank, John Hencke, (together with some family members) went to Manila with us on a Prisoner of War "Children's" Tour. He was able to give us a blow-by-blow narrative of the Flying Column's crawl through the darkened, mine-infested streets of the city as the troops tried to find the camp. A vivid description of his role as gunner on the Battlin' Basic as it approached the main gate of Santo Tomas on the night of February 3, 1945 kept us riveted.

Were we really liberated? Several hundred men had raced to Manila and had entered the camp; yet, outside there was an entire Japanese army taken by surprise. It was important that the Japanese not know how few troops had pulled off this coup.

The cavalry lost no time in setting up an armed encampment within the walls of Santo Tomas. Huge artillery guns lined the plaza. Tents, trucks, and hospital equipment were quickly set up. Reinforcements were expected soon, but bringing up the rear was the 37th Infantry Division, which was meeting much more resistance from the enemy than the first forces to enter the city. For the first couple of days, it was imperative that the small contingent in Santo Tomas maintain a low profile. There was an explosive situation to handle right within the compound.

The Japanese guards in the Education Building were housed on the lower floors. Men and boys were quartered on the upper. There were some boys in the building whose fathers were not present in the camp for various reasons and who were in the care of other men assigned to watch out for them. The Japanese decided to hold hostage the internees in this building. At first, the American soldiers not realizing that prisoners were being held there trained their guns and searchlights on the front of the building ready to do battle with the guards. With all the military maneuvering, and the firepower out in the front plaza, one would think that we would have been afraid to observe this drama that was unfolding. But we were hardened as well as curious. The soldiers warned us to stay back. The resulting standoff at the Education Building lasted for a day and a half, with many hours of tense negotiation taking place before an agreement was reached regarding the safety of the hostages and the status of the guards. Finally on the morning of February fifth, accompanied by our troops, Colonel Hayashi, the Commandant, and his men were escorted out of the camp to a prearranged spot and thereupon released.

From my diary:

February 4 Japanese in Education Building refuse to surrender and internees are on the 3rd floor. Lots of shooting. Food galore. Japanese snipers snipe our troops. Wonderful thick mush with mongo beans and corned beef. Stayed up all night again. Keep 'em Flying!

February 5 Geoffrey got a can of noodle and meat stew, one can bacon, one can cheese and one can cocoa. Walked all around the tanks and trucks. Japanese left the Ed building. Lots of Filipinos came in. Raised U.S.Flag..Old Glory.

The children roamed amongst the tanks and guns. We talked to and made friends with the soldiers. Sometimes they would have to leave with their units and go out into the city. Many times, they did not return. Within a couple of days, the reinforcements of the 37th Infantry arrived. Now the camp area was filled with thousands of soldiers, ample food supplies, hospital equipment, more armored vehicles, and big guns. The army supplied us with food as well as prepared it. Many people became sick from the richness of the rations. As children, we were given lots of candy and loads of Fig Newtons.

There was a major problem with the water supply because waterlines had been blown up. The toilets were all stopped up and overflowing. There was no water in the taps. The army brought in some portable tanks, and we filled up at these for limited use.

All the while, we were adjusting to being in an armed camp; the fighting, artillery fire, and incendiary fires continued outside the wall. We were free from our captors but not free to venture outside the walls. The safest place in Manila at that point was Santo Tomas Camp.

Safety was short lived, however. On the morning of February 7, an official ceremony was held on the main plaza. Someone had been hiding an American flag for years, and now was the time to bring this one from its hiding place and display it proudly. A group of people stood on the roof of the porte cochere overlooking the plaza, and from there, Dr. Walter Foley unfurled the Stars and Stripes while the throng assembled below waved wildly and burst into a rousing rendition of "The Star Spangled Banner."

A short time later, we were alerted to the fact that a famous visitor was about to appear in camp. An entourage rolled through the main gate and out of a staff car stepped General Douglas MacArthur, who was at once besieged by crowds of grateful ex-prisoners. Of course, he recognized some familiar faces in the crowd, and some of his cronies from the prewar days. He pushed his way through the skeleton-like, raggedly dressed sea of humanity and made his way into the Main Building and up to the second floor. This is where I managed to get near enough to him to touch his arm. It seemed that the adoring crowd just wanted to touch the imposing figure who towered above us all.

Years later, MacArthur wrote about his entrance into Santo Tomas:

I made my way to the concentration camps. I cannot recall, even in a life filled with emotional scenes, a more moving spectacle than my first visit to Santo Tomas Internment Camp. It was still under bombardment. When I arrived, the pitiful, half-starved inmates broke out into excited yells. I entered the building and was immediately pressed back against the wall by thousands of emotionally-charged people. In their ragged, filthy clothes, with tears streaming down their faces, they seemed to be using their last strength to fight their way close enough to grasp my hand. They wept and laughed hysterically, and all of them at once wanted to tell me, 'thank you'. I was grabbed by the jacket. I was kissed. I was hugged. It was a wonderful and never-to-be-forgotten moment, to be a lifesaver, and not a life-taker. (3)

Despite the accouterments of war inside the camp grounds, and the sounds of battle on the outside, the children had become quite complacent. We wandered around the huge guns, climbed over tanks and trucks, and sat in jeeps talking with soldiers who were relaxing for a few minutes before heading out for battle. On the afternoon of February 7, not long after MacArthur's visit, all hell opened up.

We children were out on the front plaza when the air above was punctuated by the screaming of a shell streaking across the sky. However, this shell was not intended for some military target. It was directed at the Main Building. In a split second, there was a violent explosion as the missile hit the corner of the building. Everyone scattered quickly, seeking cover. Some of us hit the ground, others crawled under vehicles. Still others ran for the protection of the building. This barrage of shells was the beginning of several days of constant bombardment by the enemy. One after another, the shells tore into the heavy concrete walls.

Our room, 30A, on the northeast corner was farthest away from where the shells were landing at first. Sometimes there was a lull and people went back into their rooms to retrieve belongings. At one such time, a barrage of shells struck the building on the southwest corner, and several people were killed. Among them was Dr. Foley, who that morning had raised the American flag over the camp. At another lull, some people had wandered out back, toward the eating sheds and clothes-washing troughs, thinking it was safe. A shell landed in their midst and several were killed at that location.

As the tempo of the shelling increased, we were ordered out of our rooms to the first floor. We spent the night huddled together with our backs against an inside wall. As the shells continued to hit the building, the corridors filled with acrid-smelling smoke and fumes. Great chunks of concrete fell from the ceiling onto the floor and onto those crowded there. Debris was propelled down the hallway from the force of the blasts. Windowpanes cracked and shattered everywhere. The air cleared for a time, but in moments other direct hits followed. The sound of shells striking the building was deafening. Soon, shanty areas were being hit as well.

An emergency room was set up next to where we had taken refuge to take in the wounded and dying who were brought in on stretchers by the medics. At one point, placed on the floor in front of us, was a line of stretchers bearing the casualties, both civilian and military, who were waiting for medical attention. These unfortunate souls, who just a few hours before had been celebrating their freedom, now lay gravely wounded or dying. A few were beyond help, much of their bodies having been blown to bits. The medics had not yet had time to cover the victims, and seeing the mutilated and blooded bodies before me was a scene forever etched in my mind.

The holocaust continued all night. Hundreds of us remained crowded in the downstairs hallway through the night and into the next day. If there were a break in the explosions, our relief was not long lived; a fresh barrage soon ensued. Crouched against the cement wall amidst the debris and stretchers before me, I felt certain that we would all be killed. At every strike, we hid our heads and prayed.

None of us will ever forget that night as we huddled together in the corridor amidst the chaos of fumes, smoke, rubble, falling concrete, shattered bodies, and death. It seemed as if all three years of the war were wrapped up into the horror of February seventh. A few days before, we had breathed the first air of freedom; now the reality of war made us realize how fragile that freedom was. How tenuous was the thread of existence!

We were told that some Japanese dressed as priests were found in the tower of the Main Building and were giving signals to the gunners at the artillery placements on the other side of the city. Over the next few days, the bombardment became somewhat sporadic, but no less fearsome. We went about our business uneasily, always with our ears alert to the whine of the missiles.

However, many times during the next few days, there would be periods of shellfire. Not all hit the building. Some fell in the plaza; others, in the roadways; and some, in the shanty areas. Where the shells were going to strike was unpredictable. While standing in the chow line one evening, a shell hit the building, and a piece of shrapnel lodged in the wall not far above my head. In another close call, my father and I were coming back from a hospital visit next door in the Education Building where a temporary hospital had been set up. We were just about to cross the street when a loud exploding shell pierced the air. There was a parked truck in front of us, and we both dived under it to escape the shrapnel and debris. It was some time before we got up our nerve to crawl out.

From my diary:

> February 10 Went to see Miss E and Mrs. B in the Ed building hospital. The Japanese shell the building again and I was caught at the Ed building. Terribly frightened. In leaving the building, I had to dive under a truck. Main building is hit ten times.

> February 11 Loud shelling. No water. Toilets are over-flowing.

> February 12 Mother feels sick. Awful shelling. Mother goes to hospital at nine p.m. I find medics to take her. Many tracer bullets.

As I mentioned, many people became violently ill after the initial feasting on army food. Mother was one of these. One night early in the liberation period, she woke writhing in pain. We had gotten so that we could fall asleep even with all the bombardment and tracer bullets whizzing by. Shirley stayed with Mother while I ran out into the night to find a medic. Fortunately, I found a couple right away. Mother was taken on a stretcher to the Ed Building. We were both worried about her condition; but after about three days on light food she was able to return to the room.

Outside the wall, Manila was being totally decimated. Over one hundred thousand Filipinos and other nationals met their deaths in the cruelest ways imaginable by an enemy that found itself trapped in the blazing inferno. The once beautiful, "Pearl of the Orient" lay in shambles.

Later in the month of February, as the fighting began to be less intense, we became anxious to go outside the gates and see for ourselves what lay there. One afternoon, a soldier took Mother, Shirley, and me in a Jeep over to Taft Avenue to see our old house, or, I should state, what was left of it. It had been hit many times and now lay in a heap of concrete and twisted wires. The trip took us through gutted streets, which were barely passable. Empty shells of what were once beautiful buildings, some still smoldering, lined the burned-out avenues. We wove around bomb craters. Occasionally, we'd hear the crackling of sniper bullets. It certainly wasn't "all clear," by any means. We were glad to get back to Santo Tomas.

One of the most infamous prisons in Manila was Bilibid, an old prison built in the Spanish period. Here, military prisoners, the remnants of the Bataan Death March languished. Around Christmas 1944, the Japanese moved the civilian internees from Baguio in northern Luzon and imprisoned them in a section of Bilibid. We had many friends in Baguio, and we were anxious to connect with them. An army truck was provided, and once again a driver navigated the bombed-out streets, and we were able to spend a few hours comparing notes and trading stories with old friends.

From my diary:

February 22 Had coffee with sugar. Went to Bilibid to spend the day.. Saw the Tongs. Terrific shelling in the city. Repatriation of 360 by plane.

February 23 Went out in front of Main Building to see Mr. and Mrs. Handel (from the mountains). Stood in line for shoes. No luck. Heard that Los Banos was safe and free. Terrific shelling.

February 24 Went to relief to get pajamas and pants. There was a program this morning . The 37th Infantry band played.

February 25 Thanksgiving service for liberation.

I constructed an autograph book from scraps of paper. I called it, "Autographs of Freedom." As I roamed around the camp in the days that followed our liberation, I asked many of our liberators to sign. For years afterwards I kept in contact with a few. A few years ago, I asked Hayden Rice, one of our troops who had been with an antiaircraft unit, to write what he remembered about our meeting. He was in the city of Manila on a three-day pass. He wrote me:

> When I entered the gates and saw all these people, especially the kids, I got very homesick and felt a great compassion for these people who had been Japanese prisoners. Except for the Australians in 1943, I had not seen any American or European children. They [the army] were setting up on an outside screen for a Bud Abbott, and Lou Costello movie; and on impulse, I asked the major I was with, "Let us see if we can borrow some kids and take them to the movie."
>
> On an upper floor of Santo Tomas I saw three children playing. I approached their mother and asked if she would loan me her children. She hesitated for a moment but the children said they wanted to go and she gave her permission.
>
> God bless her. She could never know how grateful I felt. We saw the movie with Geoffrey in my lap, Shirley on one side and Cecily on the other. After the movie I took the children back to their mother and before leaving, Cecily asked me to sign her autograph book with my address. It was made of scraps of paper bags as I recall. As with meeting with Mother Teresa in January 1982 at her home in Calcutta, the foregoing is one of my cherished memories. How great it has been for me to have met such wonderful people and call them my friends!

We have remained in contact all these years through correspondence and visits.

Sometimes, movies were shown by the army outside on the plaza. It was an eerie feeling, sitting and being entertained by a comedy, a musical or some irrelevant subject, while, as a backdrop for the screen, flames and smoke rising from the burning city were juxtaposed against the night sky.

We remained in the camp. There was nowhere to go in what remained of Manila. Friends from the Chinese and Filipino community visited us. Many of them recounted the horrors of the destruction of Manila and the massacre of its citizens including many of their family members.

We were anxious to see the Los Baños people who had been daringly rescued by paratroopers on the twenty-third of February.

More than two thousand prisoners were evacuated from the burning camp in amphibious vehicles that were driven across Laguna de Bay under enemy fire. The ex-internees were taken to New Bilibid, a relatively new prison and quartered there. A few days later, a bus was provided and a group of us made the trip out to the prison. I was anxious to see our Zamboanga friends who had transferred to Los Banos. From my diary:

> March 25 Ate breakfast with Arlene at Muntinlupa (New Bilibid Prison). Saw the Clingen's baby. Left on bus and saw lots of troops going to fight. Rough ride.

Meanwhile, we received mail from the States that had been piled up in some warehouse and had never been distributed. Many found out about tremendous changes that had taken place in their families during the past three years. Mother sent letters to friends and relatives to try to find a place for us to stay when we returned. The following is an excerpt from a letter I wrote to my cousin Mary while we were waiting for repatriation.

Written in Manila March 20, 1945:

Dear Mary:
What a feeling it is to be free! Words cannot express the feeling of us the night of February 3rd when the army marched in. The fires of Manila burning lit up the sky for days. We have signed up for repatriation. I have gained eighteen pounds since the Americans took Manila. I am now 89. Daddy was down to 113 and is now 146, Mother was 81 pounds and is now 97. I am afraid that if the army hadn't come when they did there would not have been many left to tell the story. Things were very bad here. Things are a million times better now and our family is well.

(1) John Mears, *John Mears, Ninety Years* (Privately Published), p.129.
(2) Samuel Eliot Morison, *The Liberation of the Philippines, Luzon, Mindanao, the Visayas 1944-1945,* (Little Brown and Company, 1975), p.194.
(3) Douglas MacArthur, *Reminiscences* (McGraw-Hill Book Company, 1964), p.247.

12 REPATRIATION

On March 25, 1945, we heard our names called on the loudspeaker for repatriation. It had been seven weeks since the liberation. Several groups of ex-prisoners had already packed up and departed by plane for Leyte, where they boarded ships for the States. There seemed to be no particular order in which anyone was called. Our family was of dual nationalities, and that usually caused a delay.

We were to be with the first group of internees who would be leaving Manila by ship instead of by plane. This explains why I have some memorabilia from those days, as we were allowed to take more with us.

On March 27, about four hundred of us were loaded onto army trucks, which then made their way down to Pier 7 in the port district. The pier had taken many bomb hits since we had seen it fourteen months previously. From my diary:

March 27 Very busy day today. We left camp at 10 a.m. on a truck. Went through the ruins of Manila to Pier 7. It looked like a bumpy caterpillar. A military band played as we got on board the army troop transport. We got Fig Newtons, gum and candy. We left at four o'clock in the afternoon and went out into the bay.

On hand to bid us bon voyage was Mrs. Douglas MacArthur and her son, Arthur.

Looking out into the bay littered with the remains of hundreds of vessels, one wondered how the *SS John Lykes* would make its way through the twisted hulks of half-sunken as well as sunken ships of every sort. These ships had been bombed, torpedoed, or scuttled during the battles to regain Manila. A minesweeper led the way. After successfully sailing through the obstacle course in the bay, we got a good look at the charred ruins of the barracks and buildings on Corregidor. There wasn't a speck of vegetation anywhere on the island. The remains of scorched trees stood silhouetted against the sky. Some monkeys were seen flitting from branch to branch and playing tag among the burnt-timbered frames of the buildings.

Once past Corregidor and the mountains of Bataan, we went below decks to our assigned quarters. Men and women were in separate sections of the ship. The area was outfitted for carrying troops, with tiers of four or five hammock-like bunks crowded together. Although fans were blowing, it was stifling hot, but at least the air moved. In addition to the ex-internees on board, there were many battle-fatigued soldiers who were returning to the States for furloughs, or maybe for the lucky few, discharge.

We were a motley-looking group, dressed in a variety of clothing: patched remnants of an outgrown prewar wardrobe, some outfits donated by the Red Cross, and a selection of mismatched donations from the army.

The ship made for Leyte on the first leg of the journey. It was in Tacloban, Leyte where we picked up a convoy of about forty ships. We needed protection as the waters were submarine and mine-infested. We were fearful, too, of a Japanese air attack. The *John Lykes* traveled in the midst of the convoy.

For the children, the days on shipboard were spent reading or playing games. A woman who had been a dance instructor organized some impromptu classes on the deck. This provided a chance to exercise and some entertainment for the onlookers. The decks were crowded, because no one wanted to be confined below. We struck up friendships with returning soldiers. It was unmercifully hot as we sailed down towards the equator. Obviously, a rather circuitous route was being taken to avoid an attack.

After about a week we pulled into Hollandia, New Guinea. Although we couldn't go ashore, we watched the activity on the docks as ships were being loaded with armor, ammunition, and troops. We children stood at the rail and tried to communicate with some of the soldiers and sailors below. Somehow we got a rope and let it down over the side, and one serviceman tied a can of lemon drops to it. We pulled it up over the rail. It certainly beat the seaweed that had been hoisted over the side of the *Shinsei Maru!* After taking on more troops and supplies, the ship pulled out into the harbor and drew up alongside a tanker for refueling. We struck up conversations with the sailors who, after being away from home for months, were anxious to talk with the women and children across the ships' rails. I passed my "Autographs of Freedom" booklet across the gap between the ships and was delighted with the signatures I added to my collection. In return, several of us received sailor hats.

From my diary:

April 6   Signed up for initiation for crossing the equator. Terrific hard rain in the afternoon. In the night there was a lot of lightning and we told ghost stories. In the morning we had dancing with Mrs. King.

April 7   We were out at sea and at 11 o'clock we anchored in Humbolt Bay opposite Hollandia. At 3 we went up to the dock. We let down a rope and a soldier sent up some lemon drops. At night we saw the movie, "Saratoga Trunk."

April 10   It is raining this morning. At noon we pull away from the docks and sail out to a tanker in the harbor. We met a nice sailor who was from Waltham, Mass. He gave us a hat and a raincoat. At six we sail away without a convoy.

We departed from Hollandia in the evening and started on our eastward journey along the equator. As we left, I stood at the ship's rail, gazing at the great dark outlines of the mountains of New Guinea that dominated the landscape, seemingly right up to the starlit heavens. I was fascinated, too, by the gentle undulating of the waves below as we plied the waters. The seas were awash with shimmering phosphorescence that seemed to replicate the twinkling of the stars above.

Our ship traveled in blackout. We sailed for several days along the equator. People began to stake out spots for themselves on top of the hatches because the heat down below was unbearable. We used the life preservers for pillows. At one point, when the ship actually crossed the equator, the crew on board had an initiation party for the children. We received certificates from King Neptune himself!

On the twelfth of April when we were somewhere in the mid-Pacific, the announcement was made that President Roosevelt had died. Other details of the death were scant.

We were a single ship crossing thousands of miles in open ocean where Japanese submarines still sought their prey. Kamikaze planes were attacking US Navy ships off Okinawa in not-too-distant waters. We were not "home free" yet.

About the thirtieth day of the voyage, we pulled into the harbor at Honolulu. Once again, we were not allowed ashore. It was here that the FBI, as well as immigration officials, came out in launches and boarded the ship. They interrogated the adults and examined papers. There were some people who had no papers, having lost them during the war. We were fingerprinted and given some official documents that allowed us to enter the United States.

Because we had traveled for more than a month without incident, we all had been lulled into a false sense of security by the time we were about five days out from the mainland. The weather was balmy. Some returned to the quarters to sleep; others stayed on deck. As a result, family units were scattered. People became careless. At the voyage's outset, we had had the customary lifeboat drill, and we were all familiar with our boat stations. Yet the thought of having to use them this close to the United States was far from anyone's mind. It was with disbelief then, when we were wakened at one o'clock one morning to the blaring of the loudspeaker announcing: "ABANDON SHIP!"

People stumbled around in the dark, moving somewhat slowly from their sleep. Then came the announcement: "CLOSE THE WATERTIGHT DOORS!" We had been told that if that announcement were forthcoming, then it was serious business. Actually, my father and Geoffrey were in the process of scrambling up the companionway from their quarters when they heard the last announcement. Mother, Shirley, and I had been sleeping on the top of a hatch across from our lifeboat station. Quickly the deck filled with swarming people, all scrambling for their places by their assigned lifeboats. Crews assigned to the lifeboats were already readying them for lowering. Quick counts were taken by frantic parents checking on their children.

I remember so well seeing the gunners climbing into their turrets, strapping themselves in, and moving the tremendous guns into position, aiming at some unidentifiable object on the horizon. Although the night was mild, we were shaking. Not a star shone overhead. As I looked to the bridge of the ship, I could see sailors sending semaphore signals out across the vast ocean. The fears that swept over me were similar to those I had had at the sound of the whine of fighter planes at the beginning of the war or during the days of shelling at Santo Tomas.

We all stood in silence wondering where the torpedo would hit and if we would soon find ourselves afloat in the Pacific Ocean just off the coast of California. Then, abruptly, the Captain announced that the emergency was over, and we could go back to quarters. As we understood it later, there was an unidentified submarine on the horizon. When the signal was given that the great guns would be fired, the submarine submerged. Some conjectured that it might have been a Japanese sub out of torpedoes on its way back to Japan. We never knew, yet it was a reminder that we were still not out of danger.

Some of the military men on board remarked later that they were amazed at the calmness with which the ex-prisoners conducted themselves and how we fell right in with what had been rehearsed with the aplomb of seasoned soldiers. In a way, we were.

Written September 24, 1945 after our return, the following describes our trip:

California Golden?

All my life I had heard about the Golden State, sunny California and wondered if that word "golden" was just a name given to her to add to her numerous other attractions.

Four hundred of us former civilian prisoners of war had sailed for more than five weeks aboard a battle-scarred army transport, escorted part way by forty other war vessels. We had come through the foreboding rocks and precipices of the straits between Samar and Leyte and passed the wilds of Mindanao. We sailed on through the Celebes Sea down to the black rolling mountains of New Guinea. As we left Hollandia, the thunderous roar of artillery faded into the past and the continuous hum of bombers dropped into memory.

The ship crept along the equator, the tropical sun beating on its decks. The graceful dolphins playfully dogged each wave, unconscious of the troubled waters in which they were frolicking.

About the third week our convoy left us, and we were alone to face the danger off Japan's coast. At one point an unidentified submarine caused the Captain to issue an Abandon Ship warning. Wasn't it enough that we had been subject to terror and starvation for three years without being left to the mercy of the far from Pacific Ocean?

On the afternoon of May third, more than a month after leaving the ravaged city of Manila, all of us were on deck scanning the water for signs of land, when like something in a dream, the rocky crags of California loomed through the blue. The sun beat on its barren cliffs. Truly to us, it was a golden land.

◆

EPILOGUE

As soon as the ship docked at the port of San Pedro, mail that had been accumulating was brought aboard. For many there was sad news. My father learned that his mother had died the year before. She was sixty-four. One couple got the news that their son, who had been sent back to the States to school, had been killed in the war in Europe. There were family changes for everyone. Arrival in America did not ensure that the future would be secure.

For us, who were met by Church representatives, the transition was smoother. Those who were met by family had an immediate sense of security. Yet, many had lost their relatives, their businesses, their property, and their money in the war. For them, although the sounds of war had been left behind, the uncertainties of building a new life lay ahead. As a result of the imprisonment, many of the group had serious medical problems, which had to be addressed before establishing a new life.

Despite the uncertainties that affected everyone in one way or another, we boarded the bus for the ride to the Red Cross Reception Center in Los Angeles. There we were extended warm hospitality and were given thorough briefings and introductions regarding the wartime regulations we were about to encounter.

Assistance was given for help in reaching relatives, help in securing medical services, and aid in making travel arrangements. In light of today's casual dress, the following entry on the information sheet we received brings a smile:

> The American Red Cross will accompany you as a guide to help make the necessary purchases of shoes, hats and <u>appropriate clothing for travel</u>.

I learned later, some people were billed by the government for the trip to the United States. Just recently, I obtained a copy of the ship's manifest of our trip on the *SS John Lykes*. Beside my father's name was the notation "paid" and also a notation granting him permission to stay here for one year. It is hard to believe that we actually had to pay for our trip after having been "rescued from enemy territory!" Who paid? We didn't have any money. All questions I wish I had asked long ago.

Goodbyes were hasty. There was a flurried exchange of addresses and farewells. For the most part, it was the last contact we had with the majority of people aboard the *SS John Lykes*; people with whom we had lived under the most trying of conditions for more than three years. Each was consumed with his or her own reentry. After a few days, we scattered across America and Canada.

Our family was met at the center by Church representatives who helped us with finances and the opening of an account at the May Company, a downtown department store. We were anxious to shed the apparel we had arrived in, the remnants of a patched and outgrown wardrobe. We were agog at what was available in the department store, even in wartime. However, Shirley and I were somewhat embarrassed later by the twin sailor dresses Mother bought for us. She was in a time warp, I guess. The dresses fit because we were undersized. We were to discover that twelve and fourteen-year-olds didn't wear sailor dresses.

Arrangements were made for our trip across the country. In Kansas City, I developed excruciating stomach pains, and a doctor had to be called aboard the train. I had turned a bright orange color, so the problem was immediately apparent. There wasn't much to do for the jaundice, but the effects of it lingered for months, and bouts recurred for years.

A college friend of Mother's loaned us her house in Lynn, Massachusetts for the summer. After a few weeks, we went up to Middlebury, Vermont to visit our grandmother who had moved there during the war. Her family had a tiny cottage on Lake Dunmore. We children stayed there at the lake with our grandmother while our parents looked for more permanent housing and figured out their next move.

The Church kept them busy with speaking engagements. The Reconstruction and Advance Fund was established for the rebuilding of the missions in the Philippines; they were fully involved in helping to make this venture a success.

With the coming of fall, it became imperative that we find a place to settle so that we children could enroll in school. It had been a year since we had been in a classroom, even one in a prison camp!

Mother was drawn to Waltham, where she had grown up and where she still had many contacts. She found a woman who had recently lost her husband and was willing to rent a portion of her large house to our family. Taking in a whole family such as ours, with a teenager and two on the way, was truly an act of kindness as well as one of bravery. We stayed for three years!

Mrs. Clarke, in whose house we lived, gave violin lessons; we had to tiptoe around so as not to disturb the pupils. A great deal of pleasure was derived from listening to the more advanced pupils, but the scratchiness of the beginners required fortitude.

We shared the one bathroom and kitchen facilities. It was an adjustment for everyone. Mother had had little culinary experience other than eking out an existence in the mountains and doctoring up the lugao in the camps. Yet, we were grateful to have a "home" at long last.

In the fall of 1945, armed with the following letter from the Chairman of the Education Department of Santo Tomas, we proceeded to enroll in schools. Excerpts include the following:

To Any Education Official Concerned:

....Improper diet at all times and the insufficiency of food during the last six months, coupled with nervousness due to war excitement, over stimulation, insufficient rest in crowded conditions, has been another adverse condition with which to deal. In addition, most of the young people over fourteen carried a regular camp work assignment of two hours while children of all ages have been needed and used for standing in food lines, laundering, carrying water, running errands, etc. in our primitive way of living. That young people have done fairly good school work in those circumstances is clear evidence of their ability to adjust to changing conditions. In other hard ways they have been trained to face life without the cushioning that modern life usually affords American and British children. It is probable that this internment experience has matured most of our students and possibly hardened some.

When this letter and these credentials are presented to you we expect you to follow your regular routine in evaluating the work and in grade placement. We do not desire the student to be advance beyond his training because that might make an academic cripple of him in the future. We do hope, however, in the light of the above circumstances, that a student from our Manila Internment Camp School will be given a fair period of probation in which to adjust to regular school procedure. Given this, we believe that most of our students will evidence that, even under strenuous conditions, they have acquired a good grasp of the work for which we have given them credit.

Shirley and I, with the help of scholarships, enrolled in Chapel Hill School a small private school a short distance from where we lived. Geoffrey went to the public school down the street. That letter of introduction was all the "cushioning" we received. There was no supporting trauma team on hand. Mother, wholeheartedly, supported the no-nonsense quick immersion method of entry into the American education system. Her attitude was, "Eat your spinach and keep quiet!" In fact, that was the attitude she adopted for herself after the war. Pick yourself up and go on. Drawing material from the war and camp, she did go out and speak to churches and service organizations on behalf of missions, but, at home, she seldom made the previous three years subjects for discussion.

As individuals, we were all affected by our experiences in different ways, but they were never used as excuses for why something couldn't be accomplished. For me, for example, there were some major gaps in my math background. Fractions and decimals had to be learned the night before a test without a whole school year being spent on tedious flash card review. The big void, educationally speaking, had its advantages!

Meanwhile my father obtained his American citizenship and made plans for a return to the Philippines as soon as he received his assignment. We all completed the paper work and necessary physicals and fully expected to follow him.

In the fall of 1946, Daddy left for Manila. We were all reluctant to see him go but expected that it wouldn't be long before we were all together. He was assigned to St. Luke's Hospital in Manila as Chaplain and also as Priest-in-Charge of the pro cathedral on the hospital grounds. (The original cathedral had been destroyed in the battle for Manila.) He also taught homiletics at St. Andrew's Seminary.

As it turned out, the Church did not want families to go out to the Philippines. It was far too dangerous. Living conditions in the city were deplorable. My father was living in a house on the hospital grounds with at least twelve others. So the rest of the family remained in Waltham. Nevertheless, fatherly advice came from across the Pacific. From a letter written to me while at summer camp in 1947:

I hope you and Shirley are being choice in the matter of friendships and cultivating the acquaintance of girls who will stimulate the best in you. A whole lot of future happiness depends on wise conduct now. Keep your mind innocent and you will walk in light and peace. Not a sermon, but advice.

From Manila he wrote:

Quite frequently I have Zamboanga visitors, mostly former school boys passing through Manila. They all look me up when they know where I am. They all want me back in Zamboanga. One fellow, Raymundo Garcia, I believe, said, "Old and young alike, they all want you back." It is very comforting of course, but quite impossible.

He goes on:

In the meantime, I am preparing lectures for the new seminary where I have charge of sermons and sermon construction plus the use of voice. I am thinking of polishing up my Greek with the object of qualifying to teach elementary ecclesiastical Greek as no one else seems qualified for this. I feel a certain "yen" for languages.

I directed a one-act play for the nursing students. The nurses are proud of my acting ability. They call me the double of Charles Laughton! I am now the official dramatic leader.

Despite being so involved with the life at the hospital, the seminary and the cathedral, in late 1948 he made the decision to return. He wrote:

> By 1948, Manila, among World War Two's most heavily devastated cities, seemed noisier, dirtier, more chaotic and hotter than ever. I was faced with one of those crucial decisions that would change my family's life in an inalterable fashion. Should I stay on in the Philippines continuing the work Mrs. Mattocks and I had been involved in since the Twenties or should I give it all up and return to the States and do parochial work? Vivid war memories mixed with the ever increasing intolerable conditions and the long separation from my family made the choice easier: Homeward Bound!

Finding a parish wasn't easy. He'd had no experience in stateside parish life. After a series of possibilities, however, he accepted a call from St. Andrew's Church in Ayer, Massachusetts. A speaking engagement at Groton School had presented this situation. After his talk, one of the masters at the school mentioned that the parish in Ayer, which at that time was a mission of the school, was vacant. No one could be found to fill the position because the rectory was right next to the busy Boston and Maine Railroad tracks; the adjacent area was occupied by double and triple deckers in need of repair, and around the corner on a side street, a very offensive-smelling tannery spewed its fumes into the air.

After our family's experiences, however, the above-mentioned impediments seemed trivial. Church members came from surrounding towns as well as Fort Devens. My father's first service was Christmas Eve 1948. He remained at St. Andrew's for the rest of his career. It was a great fit. We moved into the rectory and soon got accustomed to the freights shaking the house day and night.

People recall my father as a talented preacher. At one point the parishioners called his sermons *The Perils of Pauline,* after an early talkie movie. Always with a flair for the dramatic, he'd leave the congregation just before the climax of some exciting story, planning the next installment for the following Sunday. He knew how to fill the church.

He was known to survey the Sunday morning pews prior to the service and then send an acolyte out to change a couple of hymns on the board when he spied someone who would appreciate a rousing old favorite rather than the dirge for the day.

Mother, immersing herself in the work of the parish over the years, involved herself in the pageants, gardening around the church, playing the organ, and directing the choir. She taught full time at various area public schools. Occasionally, I would meet people who had had her as a teacher. They all report that although strict, she was the best teacher they ever had. No watered-down curriculum for her! It was hands-on. Former students remember making soap and candles as well as reading from the classics.

Taking the train right at our front doorstep, I continued with school in Waltham. It was my junior year and, having completed enough credits, it turned out to be my graduating year as well. I deferred going to Middlebury College that fall (1949) because of illness, but matriculated the next year after working at a newspaper in the interim. Prior to college, the four years I spent at Chapel Hill after our return were the only four years of schooling I was enrolled in from the beginning to the end of the school year. We had been home-schooled, participated in prison camp classes when conditions allowed, and went many months with no classes of any sort, formal or informal. One did not set out to plan this unorthodox educational program. Yet, who could have imagined or anticipated its favorable outcome? We all received an "education" that was far more valuable than the one we might have received had we not been prisoners of the Japanese. I remember looking at my first standardized test and thinking, "What's this? Just blacken in some circles!"

Living next to the tracks as we did brought some strange callers knocking at the rectory door. Hobos who rode the freights would jump off in Ayer and make their way to our door seeking handouts. Mother would have them complete some chore before she gave them a meal. Money was never doled out. There was a pair of men we kids called the "Smith Brothers" after the men on the cough drop packages. They always made a call at rummage sale time when the rummage for sale was piled up on our front porch. Since the sale was in the fall, they were usually looking for warmer clothes. Mother obliged, but not before the yard around the church had been raked of leaves.

People have asked: "Did we suffer any long lasting ill effects from the war?"

Some are disappointed when we cannot point to bodily scars. For Mother, there was a determination never to be caught short again. She would be prepared for the Russian Army. Anything. After her death, we cleaned hundreds of hardened five-pound bags of sugar out of the attic as well as scraped up the remains of bags of flour and washing detergent that an army of mice had destroyed.

She couldn't bring herself to throw anything out. We turned Christmas card envelopes inside out, ironed them, and used the clean side for scrap paper. She lost interest in fixing up a house again or amassing the trappings of a picture perfect home. The boxes and bags that were stacked by the back entry all had a reason for being there in her estimation. The rest of us might have called it "junk." Having lost all worldly goods of value once, she had no desire to invest in duplicating her prewar domicile. We were allowed one paper napkin a day. She wrote our names on a clothespin that we clipped to the napkin. My grandchildren ask "What's a clothespin?" She was piling up compost in the yard when most people didn't know what the word meant. We were allowed half a paper towel; then we hung it to dry! War neurosis? Ahead of her time?

She had time for the less fortunate, time to spend helping a student, time for the Red Cross, the hospital, and other civic organizations. When she died at eight-three, hundreds of people came to her funeral. Each of them had a story of how Dorothy Mattocks had touched their lives. This was her legacy.

My father died just before his ninety-seventh birthday, still recalling the days when he buried the captain at sea. He had survived army service in World War I, being a passenger aboard a ship that was attacked off the coast of Scotland, and World War Two as a prisoner of war. He had achieved his dream of seeing the world, surviving its pitfalls, and enjoying to the fullest all the best it had to offer.

I have been back to the Philippines several times. Zamboanga has been off limits to Western travelers for some time. I would like to have visited our mountain hideaway.

Memories will have to suffice.

Visits to St. Stephen's School have been especially nostalgic. My parents' pictures hang in their Hall of Fame. Many still remember them with fondness. I was able to view some of the artifacts that had been rescued from the burned-out church including records of services my father had taken. What is most gratifying is that St. Stephen's School today is a thriving accredited institution, proud and respectful of its past, yet not bound by it. Christian traditions still are at the forefront of its educational philosophy. The groundwork that was laid years ago has been a fertile one; the first-class institution thrives and produces students well-prepared to enter the universities to which they are admitted.

My trips to the Philippines have included visits to Santo Tomas University, having long since returned to its original status as an outstanding educational institution. On the front of the Main Building there is a plaque which reads:

Through these portals passed up to ten thousand Americans and other nationals of the free world who were interned within these walls by the Japanese military, suffering great physical privation and national humiliation from January 4, 1942 until liberated on February 3, 1945 by the American forces under General Douglas MacArthur.

Room 30A is a chemistry lab. The front of the Main Building still bears the scars of the hits it took during the shelling. The patios have been returned to places of quiet beauty.

A visit to the American cemetery inside Fort Bonifacio, where more than 17,000 American servicemen are interred, and nearby, the graves of 33,000 Filipino comrades lie buried, brings home the tremendous sacrifices that were made in the name of freedom. Across the gently undulating grassy terrain, thousands of stark white crosses stand in military formation, epitaphs to the lives that were laid down for us and thousands of others. The carillon chimes "Amazing Grace" in clear tones that are carried by the breeze across the white markers stretched out across the green landscape as far as one can see. No one speaks.

My parents seldom talked of their war experiences at home. All of us tended to go on and put those years in the past. However, with the approach of the 50th anniversary of our liberation, there was some excitement about a reunion. I was contacted by a friend who spoke about the reunion to be held in Las Vegas. I went. It was the beginning of a new chapter in the lives of those of us who shared those years behind barbed wire and iron gates. The banquet was a blazing Red, White, and Blue affair. A Forties band played a rousing rendition of "God Bless America" as we entered the banquet hall. There wasn't a dry eye anywhere. I was seeing friends I had not heard from in fifty years. Twenty or so of our liberators stood in a receiving line. They stood like giants in my memory, despite the fact that fifty years had brought them down to size.

Meeting at this emotional celebration was the nascence of a group we now call the Santo Tomas Belles. We couldn't let the years go by again without contact. How we wish we had remained connected in the intervening fifty. We were spread across the world: America, Canada, England, Australia, the Philippines. Each had her own way of picking up the pieces.

At our get-togethers, which we have held yearly since 1996, we have discovered that problems we had adjusting were not ours alone, but were in our mutual experience.

We were still at war when we returned. Some reported being appalled at teenagers swooning over the current singing idol of the day. Some found it difficult to sit through newsreels of war pictures. All our mothers, whether they had lived on expansive plantations or on mission compounds, went into the same mode. Canapes were scooped up at weddings, sugar packets were stuffed into purses, and not a scrap of food was left on a plate, ever again!

Would reentry have been easier had we remained in contact? Who knows? All of us successfully finished college despite the gaps through the years. All of us married and had children. All of us have held paying jobs. All of us are grandmothers. To an outsider, we all seem to have led perfectly average lives, even in lockstep with our peers. Yet, what we discover at our gatherings or during visits with other friends of that era is that there is a special bond that binds us. Our lives were honed and shaped by deprivation, bombs, starvation, crowded living conditions; we were witnesses to events which were difficult to reconcile with the life that lay ahead. But reconcile we did. Most of us have faced the problems, the joys, the disappointments, the excitement, and heartbreak that comes with living. How we have dealt with these issues, however, has been measured against the background of what we experienced long ago. We learned at an early age to pick ourselves up and go on.

SURVIVORS' SCRAPBOOK

It has been said that one picture represents a thousand words. Fortunately, I have been able to preserve the collection of personal and press photographs which, arranged in chronological order, reflect our family's experiences before, during and after World War II. We, like barbed wire, were caught at random intervals, but the twisted spiked knots failed to hold us captive and over time, seemed to change into the stars of a peaceful night sky, as represented on the cover of this SURVIVORS' SCRAPBOOK.

JEOFELA INTRODUCES ME TO
FEATHERED FRIENDS

CAROLINA KEEPS ME
OCCUPIED

OUR HOUSE AT 606 TAFT AVENUE, MANILA

OUTSIDE OUR NIPA PLAYHOUSE AT 606

SHIRLEY AND I WELCOME BABY BROTHER GEOFFREY

OUT FOR A SPIN WITH MOTHER IN THE MODEL A

ON THE LAWN AT TAFT AVENUE WITH OUR AMAH SERAFINA AND HER
INFANT SON BERNARD

HERE I AM WEARING A TRADITIONAL TWO-PIECE PHILIPPINE
DRESS WITH BUTTERFLY SLEEVES.....
A RED HIBISCUS COMPLETES THE OUTFIT

THE MEDICAL STAFF OUTSIDE BRENT HOSPITAL, ZAMBOANGA....
LOUISE GOLDTHORPE, HEAD NURSE,
IS AT CENTER....DR. JULIO TROTA IS AT FAR RIGHT

THE GENERATIONS FOLLOW: ZAMBOANGA PLAYMATE REMY TROTA JOSE
SEATED
AT TABLE IN CENTER SURROUNDED BY HER FAMILY...BOHOL 2007

ZAMBOANGA WATERFRONT SCENES

WE THREE KIDS IN TRADITIONAL FILIPINO CLOTHING

NIPA HUTS ALONG THE
SHORE SIMILAR TO
THE MALAYAL
SHORELINE

HANDCRAFTED
"SILVERWARE"
AND
COCoNUT SHELL
BOWL MADE
BY MY FATHER

212

TOP: MY WOODEN BAKyA
MIDDLE: MOTHER'S SHOE MADE FROM TIRE TREADS AND BITS OF CANVAS
BOTTOM: DADDY'S SANDAL MADE FROM TIRE TREADS AND RUBBER STRIPS

MANILA INTERNMENT CAMP
INTERNEE COMMITTEE

No. 42

Date Aug. 6   1944

RECEIVED from MATTOCKS, Henry

the sum of TWO HUNDRED AND SIXTY-ONE ONLY
(Japanese Military Notes)

to be used for the purchase of Supplementary Food and other essential supplies for General Welfare purposes deemed necessary by the Internee Committee.

P 261.00

_____   _____
Chairman   FINANCE DIVISION
Philippine Red Cross (ANRC)

COMMONWEALTH OF THE PHILIPPINES
PROVINCE OF DAVAO
DAVAO

...STIGATION ON HOOKWORM AND OTHER INTESTINAL PARASIT...

	AVERAGE NUMBER OF OVA PER MICROSCOPIC FIELD (?)				
HOOK-WORM		TRICH-URIS	OXYURIS	OTHER TESTI PARAS

R-E-P-O-R-T   C-A-R-D

DAVAO C. C. SCHOOL

Name   CECILY MATTOCKS

Grade   SENIOR   Year 1943-44

	July	Aug	Sept	Oct		
Spanish	95	81	80	82		
Arithmetic	87*	85*	90*	91		
English	95	92	90	90		
U.S. History	92	90	88	93		
Gen. Average	94	87½	86	90		
Art			92	90		
Phys. Culture	90	92	94	91		
Singing	95	70	95	95		
Conduct	85	90	90	90		

* Outside Regular Classes

N. B. 70% is the passing mark

Edward C. Godon...
Principal

INP SOUNDPHOTO
F-69-WATCH YOUR CREDIT.....INTERNATIONAL NEWS
SLUG (SANTO TOMAS INTERNMENT CAMP)
A GLIMPSE OF INTERNEES LIFE AT SANTO TOMAS
MANILA, P.I.......THIS SCENE WAS MADE IN THE PATIO
OF THE SANTO TOMAS UNIVERSITY INTERNMENT CAMP WHERE
SOME 400 INTERNEES COOKED MEALS AND LIVED. RUDELY
CONSTRUCTED "NIPA" HUTS COVER THE ___ INED AREA WHERE
MANY OF THE PRISONERS LIVED ___
BY THE JAPS. TROOPS OF ___ ___ IR INTERNMENT
ENTERED THIS SECT ___ ___ DIVISION
THE INT ___

SERVICE des PRISONNIERS de GUERRE
俘虜郵便

NAME_____

NATIONALITY_____

PHILIPPINE INTERNMENT CAMP NO._____

TO:_____   IMPERIAL JAPANESE ARMY

_____   1. I am interned at Philippine Internment Camp No._____

_____   2. My health is — excellent; good; fair; poor.

_____   3. Message. (Limited to 25 words.)

_____

_____

_____

_____
                                              Signature

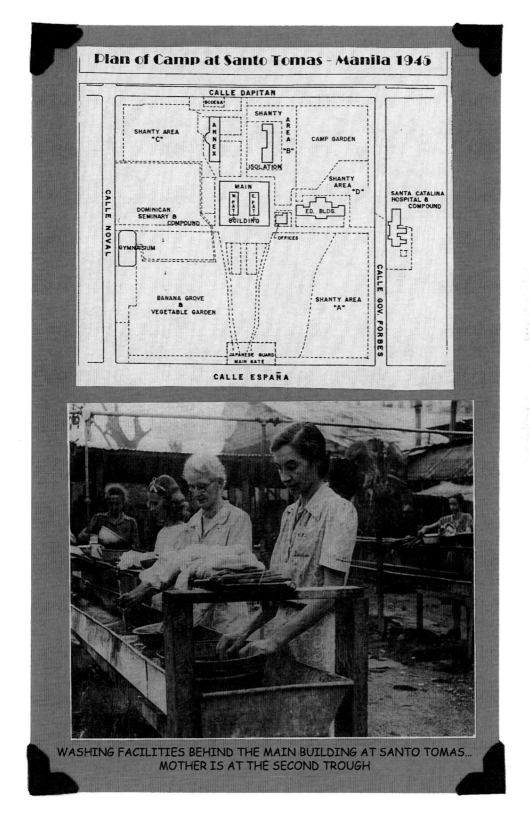

Plan of Camp at Santo Tomas - Manila 1945

CALLE DAPITAN

BODEGA

SHANTY AREA "B"

SHANTY AREA "C"

ANNEX

CAMP GARDEN

ISOLATION

MAIN BUILDING

W. PAT / E. PAT

SHANTY AREA "D"

ED. BLDG.

SANTA CATALINA HOSPITAL & COMPOUND

DOMINICAN SEMINARY & COMPOUND

OFFICES

GYMNASIUM

CALLE NOVAL

CALLE GOV. FORBES

BANANA GROVE & VEGETABLE GARDEN

SHANTY AREA "A"

JAPANESE GUARD MAIN GATE

CALLE ESPAÑA

WASHING FACILITIES BEHIND THE MAIN BUILDING AT SANTO TOMAS...
MOTHER IS AT THE SECOND TROUGH

217

...ent down to sup. 1/4 of it was gone. Stolen! Feb 3 A Jap came in room + did windows. Something up. Total Blackout. At 9:30 American tanks, trucks, troops rolled in gate. Happiest night of our lives. Didn't sleep. Feb 4 (Sun.) got asleep. Awake all night. Japs in Ed Bldg refused to surrender + internees in 3rd floor. Lots of shooting. Food galore. Jap snipers snipe our troops + Wonderful! Thick mush, mongolian stew, corned beef, mash. Stayed up all night. Mac column coming in. "open" please?

Feb. 5 (Mon.) Geoffrey got 1 can noodle + meat stew 2 cans meat + vegetable ration. 1 can bacon, cheese, cocoa. Walked all around tanks + trucks. Lots of Filipinos came in. Saw an amphibian. Japs captured. Foodstuffs came in. Lots of shooting and Planes. Raised the U.S. Flag Old Glory.

Feb. 6 (Tue.) Got life savers from a nice captain. Japs hit building once. Talked w/ Jake a funny soldier

Feb. 7 (Wed.) Japs hit building 6x. Lots of casualties & deaths. Dr. Foley killed. Slept in back lobby. Mrs. Foley had her arm amputated. Life savers in canteen. (Mac Auther came in camp.) I shook hands w/ him. Crowds crowded around him. (= before shelling.)

Feb. 8 (Thu.) Nabelle yet 3-5 deaths. Got life savers & magazines in canteen. Had bread for lunch + asparagus soup. Registered. US shell Jap positions. Had stew milk & sliced apples for sup. 159 wounded 25 deaths in STC

Feb. 9 (Fri.) Slept upstairs in room. Had can milk, 2 scoops sugar, mush, coffee + fruits. For lunch, Bread Butter + stew Supper we had. Stew + apples bread cheese butter figs milk for. "pill" Sat out w/ a soldier. Mac Auther

Feb. 10 (Sat.) Went to see Miss Earl + Mrs. Burt. Japs shell building again. Hit tower, Ed. building, shanty, + water tanks. I was caught at Ed Building. Terribly frightened. Had 2 slices of bread peach jam + stew for lunch. For supper, meat, creamed peas, bread + butter. Got Chocolate. Finished pop + wore them. Hit bldg. 6 x.

Feb. 11 (Sun.) Doesn't seem like Sunday. Loud shelling. No water

Tues. -5 Nice sunny morn. Lymegut came with bananas. Bongalo Boys came with bananas. Papaya clean. I got up in the afternoon and went for a walk with Shirley. Indian brought eggs. For supper we had the left over roast. The "GO" signs up on bananas.

Wed #6 I have no fever today so I got up. We had hash for breakfast. Shirley Geoffrey and I went to the "Woodlands" to find wood for a rack that mummy wants made. We got a lot done because no one came. Cleaned suitcase. Today is very HOT Drying.

Thurs. - 7 One year ago since we saw Zamboanga. It is a very windy morning. Blewits the paper all over the place. We cleaned the big bedroom. My it was so dirty. The shelves look much better. I don't feel very well. Geoffrey and I went to the "woodlands" to get some wood. I went to Jemima to see if I could get a little patoty made for Shirley but it was too expensive. to ask Nacida

Tues. - 12 Windy. Carabaos came last night and ate our oat meal mat. For Breakfast we finished our oat meal that was left. Daddy opened one can of Bear Brand milk because no cocoanut milk comes. Mr. Gulhansen back looking for Mr. ... He says he has to go to Zamboanga to be with Mr. and Mrs. ... by night going to ...

Wed. - 13 Last night was the worst wind we ever had. I couldn't sleep a bit. Mabye it does not want to go. Minnie laid an egg. Blueberry laid an egg. Mother puts on the oven bakes Chocolate cake. Uses up last of cake flour. Mr. Spread went. We four Shirley Geoffrey Daily mummy slept in the bed. Not much wind. But RAIN. Papaya tree fell.

Thurs. - 14 Hahndelos bed fell. Us children were laughing very much. Because we could hear it keep cracking. and kept jumping up whenever it did. Mother kept telling us to lie down, but we just couldn't. Finally with a klop it fell - Laughter was great. We stayed buy the fire. Had 2 meals only. supper was good. Daddy finished fixed bed We finished reading "Midsummer night dream".

EXCERPTS FROM MY MALAYAL DIARY

THE CATHEDRAL OF ST. MARY AND ST. JOHN...PREWAR MANILA

REMAINS OF THE CATHEDRAL DESTROYED BY SHELLING DURING
THE BATTLE FOR MANILA,
FEBRUARY 1945

ST. STEPHEN'S CHINESE CHURCH DESTROYED BY SHELLS, FEBRUARY 1945

SHELLFIRE DESTRUCTION...SANTO TOMAS MAIN BUILDING,
FEBRUARY 1945

BOYS CLAMBER OVER LIBERATORS' TANKS PARKED IN FRONT PLAZA OF SANTO TOMAS

POST LIBERATION PLAZA SCENE....DADDY IS SECOND FROM RIGHT

224

Juan Thompson
Murray Ky
Route 3

John R Taft
Sequeny zone

Gerald Hazeltine
6105 Miller Ave.
Gary, Indiana.
Sgt. H Young - Chicago, Ill
Signal Corps Photographer

T/Sgt Henry Palm
San Antonio Texas
Signal Corps Photographer

James C. Barrett
TRAC mgr FPO 201
% Post Master
San Francisco
California

John P Robson
Burlington Wyoming

J. H. Fellow
..., D.C.

AUTOGRAPHS
OF
FREEDOM

CECILY MATTOCKS

HEADQUARTERS
UNITED STATES ARMY SERVICES OF SUPPLY

APO 707
23 March 1945

Pursuant to instructions contained in letter, Headquarters USAFFE, dated 4 March, 1945, file FEGARP 704, subject: "Civilians Recovered from Enemy Occupied Territory," the bearer, MATTOCKS, MARGARET, has obtained CIC and medical clearance and has been placed on orders for evacuation to the United States.

MAX W. PEMBERTON,
Major, Inf.,
. Asst. Adj. Gen.

JOHN LYKES
6-7-41 ...

225

I TOOK THIS PICTURE AT THE AMERICAN CEMETERY, MANILA, 2000

FREEDOM'S PRICE

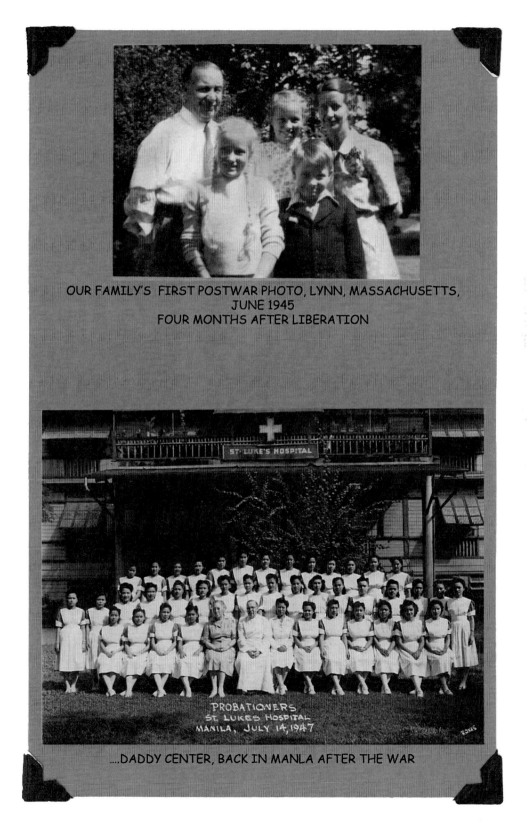

OUR FAMILY'S FIRST POSTWAR PHOTO, LYNN, MASSACHUSETTS,
JUNE 1945
FOUR MONTHS AFTER LIBERATION

....DADDY CENTER, BACK IN MANLA AFTER THE WAR

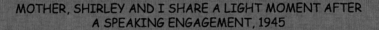

MOTHER, SHIRLEY AND I SHARE A LIGHT MOMENT AFTER
A SPEAKING ENGAGEMENT, 1945

STEPHANIAN GAZETTE

MARCH 2000.

Mrs. C. Marshall, Unveils Mattocks Collection Marker

Gazelle Anne Ngotianhe & Marlon See

Mrs. Cecily Marshall unveiled the Mattocks Collection marker, Feb. 17 at St. Stephen's High School elementary library.

The said collection includes books such as Time Life Encyclopedia, Webster International Encyclopedia, Charlie Brown Encyclopedia, 365 Bedtime Stories, Satellite Atlas of the World and cassette tapes. They also furnished the school with annual subscription of Cricket and Spider magazines.

Mrs. Marshall is the daughter of Mrs. Dorothy Mattocks, formerly Miss Dorothy Latham. She first came at St. Stephen in 1924 as a teacher, then became a principal. She married Rev. Henry Mattocks, former assistant priest of St. Stephen parish who then became the school chaplain.

SERAFINA AND PEDRO
OLIVAREZ CELEBRATE 50
YEARS OF MARRIAGE

MY GODMOTHER,
TY TAN JIN TEK

OCTOBER 2000, MACARTHUR MUSEUM, NORFOLK, VIRGINIA...

SOME Of THE SANTO TOMAS BELLES PICTURED IN FRONT OF
AN EXHIBIT OF ARTIFACTS FROM SANTO TOMAS.
THE BLOUSE IN THE UPPER LEFT CASE WAS SIGNED BY
SOME OF US EITHER IN CAMP OR ON THE *SS JOHN LYKES*.

PICTURED STANDING FROM LEFT TO RIGHT: SHERRY LEWIS NEWKIRK;
ISABEL COGAN KREBS; ANN LEWIS CONROY; DERRY MILLS DEAN;
DOLLY ROGERS CLEMENS; LOUISE HOWARD HILL;
CECILY MATTOCKS MARSHALL; ROBERTA OLSEN SLIVON.
SEATED: SASCHA WEINZHEIMER JANSEN

Glossary

amah: nursemaid
am pao be: puffed rice candy
bakya: a wooden slide-like clog
balut: embryonic duck egg
banca: outriggered boat
benjo: toilet facilities (Japanese)
bibingka: a "cake" made of rice flour, sugar, and coconut milk baked in a banana leaf
bodega: warehouse
bolo: machete
bucayo: coconut candy
calamanci: lime
calesa: horse drawn coach-like vehicle for transporting people
camote: sweet potato
carabao: water buffalo
caromata: same as calesa
cassava: a root vegetable
cawa: large cast iron vat
chico: a small brown fruit with black seeds
Datu: Moslem tribal chieftain
dilis: tiny dried fish
gabi: taro
junk: flat-bottomed sailing ship (Chinese)
juramentado: (from the Spanish) to swear, or to take an oath
kangkong: pigweed
kaingen: a barren mountainside planted with crops of camotes or corn, usually
Kempeitai: Japanese military police
kris: a long sword
lanzone: small fruit with clove-like sections
lavandera: laundress
lugao: boiled rice of a mush-like consistency

masarap: delicious
mestizo/a: of mixed races
Moro: collection of tribal groups united by a common religion–
    Islam
nipa: palm frond
palay: unhusked rice
pantalan: pier
pechay: kind of cabbage
petate: straw mat
piña: a delicate fabric, a material made from the pineapple plant
pomelo; similar to a grapefruit
sala: living room
sampaguita: fragrant tiny white flower, Philippine national
    flower
sampan: flat-bottomed skiff (Chinese)
sawali: woven bamboo
STIC: Santo Tomas Internment Camp
talinum: similar to spinach-slippery
tienda: store
tomaru: halt (Japanese)
tuba: a drink from fermented coconut sap

ACKNOWLEDGMENTS

I am indebted to those who through the years prodded me to write "my" story. It took some time to gather the bits and pieces of the writings which other family members and I had already put to paper. My "emergency suitcase" containing wartime memorabilia had been gathering dust in its storage place under a bed. But apart from the massive hunt for material and years of procrastination, there were certain people who contributed invaluably to the completion of HAPPY LIFE BLUES once I decided to go forward.

Special thanks to:

Tom Bartlett for encouraging me to record the experience.
Dr. Lorenzo Campos who refreshed my memory of Tagalog vocabulary.
Dr. Rico Trota Jose for some historical perspective.
Dr. James Hopkins for the reel to reel taping of my father's recollections.
Deena Madnick for her editorial assistance.
Cynthia Hall Marshall for the cover design and lay-out.
Kathleen Kloss Marshall who patiently photographed the "artifacts."
Nancy Connor Marshall for daring to correct her mother-in-law's initial efforts.
Dr. Tiu Uy Pei Suan who brought me up to date on St. Stephen's School.
James Zobel for supplying archival photos from the MacArthur Museum.

I also extend appreciation to the many others who willingly shared recollections, photographs and portions of their diaries.

Finally I owe a debt of gratitude to my husband **Peter** and my children **Jonathan, Kristin, Bruce, and Stephen** who offered constant support and encouragement.

BIBLIOGRAPHY

Cary, Frank. *Letters from Internment Camp, Davao and Manila, 1942-1945.* Independent Printing Company, Ashland (Oregon): 1993.

Hammer, Joshua. *Yokohama Burning.* Free Press: London, 2006.

Hartendorp, A.V.H. *The Santo Tomas Story.* McGraw-Hill Book Company: New York, 1964.

Klestadt, Albert. *The Sea Was Kind.* Kangaroo Press, Pty, Ltd.: Singapore, 1959, 1988.

MacArthur, Douglas. *Reminiscences.* McGraw-Hill Book Company: New York, 1964.

Mears, John D. *John Mears, Ninety Years.* Privately Published, 2002.

Morison, Samuel Eliot. *The Liberation of the Philippines, Luzon, Mindanao, the Visayas. 1944-1945,* Little Brown and Company, Boston, 1975.

Stahl, Alfred J. *How We Took It.* New York: Privately Published, 1945.

Stevens, Frederic H. *Santo Tomas Internment Camp.* Limited Private Edition, 1946.

PHOTO CREDITS

HAPPY LIFE BLUES

Chapter 10—*Last Days* -Cook shanties in the Patio, Santo Tomas. Courtesy of the MacArthur Memorial Archives, Norfolk, VA. US Army Signal Corps photo.

Chapter 11—*Liberation*-Internees cheering the flag raising. Courtesy of the MacArthur Memorial Archives. US Army Signal Corps photo.

Chapter 12—*Repatriation*-Dockside at Pier 7 preparing to board the SS *John Lykes*. Courtesy of MacArthur Memorial Archives. US Army Signal Corps photo.

SURVIVORS' SCRAPBOOK

PAGE 208—Photos, courtesy of Remedios Trota Jose.

PAGE 209—Boys in bancas and vinta with Moro fishing village in background, courtesy of Peter Parsons.

PAGE 215—Scenes from the East Patio, photo courtesy of Turner Publishing Company, LLC, Paducah, KY.

PAGE 215—Description of patio scene, courtesy of the MacArthur Memorial Archives, US Army Signal Corps photo.

PAGE 217—Women at the washtubs, courtesy of the MacArthur Memorial Archives, US Army Signal Corps Photo.

PAGE 223—Shell destruction at Santo Tomas, photo courtesy of Turner Publishing Company, LLC, Paducah, KY.

PAGE 224—Top: Boys on tanks, courtesy of the MacArthur Memorial Archives, US Army Signal Corps.

PAGE 224—Bottom: Scene of ex-internees in plaza, from The First Cavalry Division in World War II, Major B.C. Wright, 1947.

PAGE 225—The SS *John Lykes* , courtesy of the MacArthur Memorial Archives, US Army Signal Corps photo.

BACK COVER

Patio scene, courtesy of the MacArthur Memorial Archives,US Army Signal Corps photo.

ABOUT THE AUTHOR

Cecily Mattocks Marshall
lives in West Boylston and Sandwich, Massachusetts
with her husband, Peter. She is the mother of four and
grandmother of fifteen. A graduate of Middlebury
College in Vermont, she taught school for many years,
most recently in the Clinton, Massachusetts Public
School System where she served as Coordinator of
the Bilingual Educational Department.